SEND F   RS
TO THE LIVING!

Rewards, Contests and Incentives to Build Employee Loyalty

T.J. Schier

RECRUIT
TRAIN
REWARD
RETAIN.
Incentivize
Solutions

I would like to "send some flowers" to the following people:

My family: Sue, Courtney and Matthew for having unwavering support, faith and love.

My parents and brother for always being supportive in everything and providing great direction, guidance and love.

Jim Sullivan, for mentoring me through the self-employment and book-writing processes.

Copyright © 2002 TJ Schier

Published by:
Incentivize Solutions
PO Box 271170
Flower Mound, TX 75027
(972) 691-7378

Printed in the United States of America by Banta Book Group

Schier, TJ 1966-
     Send flowers to the living!   : rewards, contests and incentives to build employee loyalty / TJ Schier.

     ISBN 0-9716573-0-0

     1. Business Management

Library of Congress Control Number: 2001099336

Cover design, illustration and book layout:
CLICK! Visuals, Inc.– (800) 490-3210, www.clickvisuals.com

Edited by:
Donna Pekkonen

TABLE OF CONTENTS

IT'S NOT FUN IF NOBODY IS CLAPPING!

There is a story about a little girl who received a jump rope as a gift. She absolutely loved it and took it everywhere. One Sunday, she talked her mom into letting her bring it to church. After the service, the mom was talking to a group of adults and the girl kept asking to show everyone how good she was. Mom gave in and the girl put on a show. When she was finished, everyone gave her an ovation and many words of praise. The mom then directed her to play "over there" until she was finished talking to her friends. A short while later the girl returned. Her mom asked why she stopped jumping rope. Her reply? *"It's not fun if nobody is clapping!"* Think about that the next time one of your employees is doing some of their daily tasks.

The most underutilized motivator is recognition. Why? To most people, it isn't *natural.* Since people tend to manage the way they get managed, most managers today only focus on what their people do wrong. It seems with today's light-speed pace, only the best companies and managers actually take time to slow down and recognize the people that truly drive their business. Everyone has worked in situations where "no news is good news." Do you manage your people any differently?

Turnover in corporations has reached staggering levels. Employees change companies far more frequently than previous generations. In the service industry, it is quite common to see hourly employee turnover rates in excess of 200%! Managers are constantly looking to keep costs in line, drive productivity and save money – at the short-term expense of their people, and the long-term expense of their company. Even worse, when they realize they have a turnover problem, one typically hears:

"It is so hard to find good help."

"People just are not like they used to be."

"Kids/people today."

"The competition is paying more."

FOREWORD

They go for instant fixes that just don't work. In most cases, it is not a *HIRING* problem, but a *RETENTION* problem. Most places of business have plenty of applications or resumes; they just can't keep the employees they have. More and more dollars are thrown at recruiting new people through the revolving door. Well, it is time to STOP that cycle!

The ability to keep employees satisfied is the foundation for running a successful business. Many of the leaders in business today have proven time and time again that there is a direct correlation between employee satisfaction and key business indicators such as sales increases, profitability, guest satisfaction scores and labor cost containment. If you look at the most admired companies in this country, management tracks turnover, people are compensated on the turnover of their direct reports and their turnover is minimal when compared to their competitors. Not only do they save a significant amount of money on the recruiting and training side, they provide a consistent experience for their guests/customers/clients that undoubtedly drives top line sales and bottom line profits.

Parents do a great job encouraging and rewarding their children, especially when they are young, to learn and accomplish new things. Somewhere along the line, however, that gets managed out of many people. That's when the "no news is good news" management style becomes prevalent.

Picture a game of soccer played by 4-6 year olds. Parents are beyond supportive, cheering even the most minor of attempts by the team on the field. How much fun would it be if we did not cheer (i.e. like most people manage)? Think the kids would want to keep playing? Doubtful. The work environment should be no different. If we honestly expect employees to do their jobs at a high level and never hear any "clapping" we are fooling ourselves.

Knowing the problem and actually doing something about it are two different things. Creating a recognition culture to strengthen personal relationships within your organization will create lasting value. Read on to learn how and then commit to doing the things described here. Changing a culture (depending on the size of the organization) can take a couple of months or years. Many are hesitant to undertake those changes. And not every investment pays an immediate return. The only way to truly make money in the business world is to have a long-term approach.

That same approach must be taken with your people. Invest often (like reinvesting dividends in a stock) and watch the incredible payout over time – it works in finance and it works with people. You have to be committed to the short-term sacrifice - delivering praise or paying out small amounts for rewards (like forgoing cashing a dividend check and using the money now). Don't let this be just another 'fad' that you try for a short while. That flicker of light will be blown out by the rigors of the daily grind unless you truly commit to making the new change stick. Not many people can say they have made a true, lasting impact on a company and peoples' lives – you can if you choose to commit to the methods outlined here.

If you always focus on the needs of the company, you will miss the employees' fundamental needs (the foundation of the relationship with their boss). Everyone knows what happens to relationships that do not have a solid foundation. Build a high level of trust with your employees and ensure they 'fit-in' at your company. Meeting their basic needs of compensation, benefits, a solid relationship with their boss and peers will ensure they will be fully committed to implementing the corporation's objectives and fulfilling the mission of the business. Providing an environment that recognizes people's accomplishments and values their input and worth will create a place that fosters sales and profit building to ensure you achieve your vision.

A few notes before moving into the book:

- Recognition is NOT a program. While there are some contests and programs described within this book, those alone will not create a long-term recognition culture within your organization. Too often, managers are always looking for the 'quick-fix' or 'silver bullet'. They don't exist! These contests are simply pieces of a bigger puzzle that need to be put together to ensure you have the premier work environment for your employees. They can help jumpstart the process and get people excited about the potential of earning some additional perks.

- Portions of this book discuss spending time with your best performers. Do not interpret this the wrong way, by disregarding non-performance or violations of the rules and policies within your company. You cannot ignore non-performance or sub-standard employees.

- For ease of understanding, many of the examples throughout the book are from the service and hospitality industry. While you may not work in a service environment, you've undoubtedly been on the guest side of the equation (i.e. eating at a restaurant, shopping at a retail store), so the concepts will be easy to understand. You can then translate them into your business environment to apply them.

- Trainers, marketers and managers can use this approach to ensure training and product/procedure implementations take effect quicker and last longer by ensuring rewards and recognition tied to continued performance and focus on the objectives – make it stick! After all, how often have you heard someone in the marketing or training field say, "We had a great program, but ops/sales didn't execute." If that is the case, tie some incentives to their participation. After all, what the guest or client experiences is what matters the most – not the actual program itself.

Read on to unleash the power of "Send Flowers to the Living!" in your organization.

PLANTING THE SEEDS

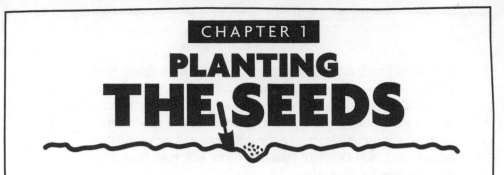

Why the title of the book? When does most recognition happen? In a company, as in personal relationships, it typically occurs on the front-end (i.e. when they are brand new), as well as when someone departs or the relationship is over. Why wait until someone leaves (or has threatened to) to 'send flowers'? How often have you heard at a person's eulogy how great they were, how many charitable things they did, how giving they were and on and on? Unfortunately, that person is no longer with us to hear those words. Many people also add, "I never got to tell ____ how I really felt." Whether it's in your personal or professional life, don't wait! You can prevent a large percentage of your employees from leaving, but it will require you to learn and implement these ideas.

The title simply means you should keep recognizing employees while they are still with you. Don't wait until they're gone from your organization. While this may seem very 'common-sense' to you, it's not a common practice. Exploit your competitors' lack of focus on their employees and make this a competitive advantage of yours. "Incentivize" is my term for providing someone a reward or incentive for achieving business goals or levels of performance.

On a recent trip to the grocery store to purchase flowers for my Mom, my Dad heard the comment from a fellow shopper: "Whoa! *Someone* did something wrong!" Since when do we only give flowers when we do something WRONG? Today's business environment and culture should not only allows us, but *encourage* us to buy flowers (give recognition) when people do things RIGHT! The same approach can be used to strengthen personal relationships – spouses, children, friends and families.

In business as in life, recognition and training is very front- and back-end loaded. While it's not quite as dramatic as death (although it certainly could be), if someone leaves your group we generally don't realize what we have until it is gone. By then, it is too late for recognition and we are forced to undertake the process (and cost) of replacing a star performer.

This approach is a call to change the way people manage/lead and deal with employees, so we create a recognition culture within an organization to ensure employees perform at their best. Driving employee loyalty is the key to creating a dynasty in your industry. Focus on (and reward) those who are performing (your stars). The process will pave the road to your success as a manager or as a company. Start the recognition now.

Individually, the ideas in this book will not change your company's culture by themselves. Collectively, if practiced throughout the organization, however, it will become a competitive advantage. You will be able to create a brand identity as an employer and be able to attract, and more importantly, retain the best people in your respective industry.

The premise is simple: Everyone in business has three main objectives:

1) Build Sales
2) Make Money
3) Grow Your People

Dick Frank, CEO and Chairman of the Board of CEC Entertainment (parent company of Chuck E Cheese's Pizza and one of the best performing stocks since going public in 1989), puts it this way, "The only true objective of business is sales." You cannot generate profits without sales. You cannot build sales without people. The culture of your organization will determine if people stay or not. Keep the good employees to drive sales over the long-term.

These three components make the company move in the right direction. If one part is not working, the tire is flat. With a flat tire, the company cannot proceed forward. The problem most companies and their managers run into is trying to balance the three objectives. The short-term decision (under Wall Street pressure or personal gain) to drive profitability often is at the expense of people development or long-term sales growth.

The same can be said for any other portion of the wheel. If you decide to sell products at a huge discount, you will drive sales but damage profitability and, in turn, impact people. Focusing on people without generating returns for the company is also detrimental. No different than discounting sales at the expense of profit, you could also spend endlessly on people development. Again, you would dramatically impact the profitability of the company if those dollars weren't spent on items that generated a financial return.

The beauty of employing this management approach is that you will focus on growing your people by rewarding them for driving sales and profits (as well as any other business objective you are working on). One part of the wheel will feed the other two and you will create an incredibly strong cycle. Therefore, you have to reward and develop the people that are generating the sales and profitability for the company for the wheel to continue rolling – and picking up momentum. Allow your employees to share in a 'fraction of the action' and drive your business forward.

In a nutshell, focus on **rewarding your performers**. Your employees will repeat what they see getting measured and rewarded. Make them feel appreciated for their input and they will stay and grow – along with your top and bottom line. Once you gain their trust and loyalty, you will have a much better chance (than your competition) of building sales and generating long-term profits.

TOP LINE – SALES

FRONT LINE
EMPLOYEE
BEHAVIORS/
TRAINING &
COSTS

BOTTOM LINE – PROFIT

SALES IS THE TOP LINE, PROFIT IS THE BOTTOM LINE.

What happens in between is driven by your frontline.

Before you read on, quiet the cynical voice in your head that is saying "yeah, but this costs money to do." Each time you hear that thought pop into your head, remember:

"Don't trip over dollars to pick up pennies!"

While it may be an old saying, it is a fundamental belief of this program. Don't get stuck on the cost of these items or programs (the pennies). Great leaders focus on 'big rock' items. Focus on the BIG dollars you will be picking up in the form of increased sales and profits, as well as reduced costs in the areas of recruiting, training and turnover.

EVOLUTION OF THE PROGRAM

I've been fortunate to learn from some of the greatest leaders in the service and training fields. Their practices have been implemented and created sales, profit and retention increases for many companies. Over the course of four years, I tested and refined the ideas outlined in this book – and made the mistakes so you won't! For you, it's an opportunity to learn what ideas drive success and the pitfalls to avoid. While many books preach theories on this subject or simply list countless ways to reward people, my approach is different. Not only will you learn '**why**,' you will also learn '**how**.'

In the mid-90's, while at the CHART (Council of Hotel and Restaurant Trainers – **www.chart.org**) Conference in Sandestin, FL Jim Sullivan 'lit the blowtorch' as he likes to say. Jim (**www.sullivision.com**) is the leading speaker and consultant in the area of guest service in the hospitality and retail industry. He spoke about suggestive selling – a topic we desperately needed in our organization.

After seeing Jim's presentation, I was sure we could make millions in our company. We tried the typical training approach – a new video and manual, roll out meetings and…THUD! A few people took off with it, but most did not. What went wrong? Why couldn't we get our people to sell? We've all been through this situation as managers – our ideas and changes are met with resistance and lack of success. Often times, we just give up and try something else. The idea was then born to try a contest to see if we could move the needle.

I put together a suggestive selling contest that rewarded employees and managers. ZOOM! Sales went up to the tune of $900,000 in 250 units over a 3-month period. Even more impressive was the fact that we saw only a slight decrease in performance once the contest ended. The contest continued to pay off even after it was over! Additionally, employee turnover went down 20%. Drive sales, increase profit and reward your people – the name of the game. With feedback from our managers and employees, we continued to improve the systems and results.

We tried many different contests, prizes and formats. Some were incredibly successful, others less so. Pay close attention while you are reading. You will see the key ideas to implement within your organization and avoid mistakes that others have made. As a reminder: one contest will not change the culture of your company – it is a process. Contests or incentive programs will get the ball rolling (and make it easier to convince top management since there is a financial payoff).

This approach focuses on a POSITIVE way to ensure your employees do what YOU want simply by rewarding them with what THEY want. It's a dramatic shift from the way your competitors manage. Here is an example:

TURN THE BRICK AROUND!
(Shift your point of view)

Schools wrestle with attendance problems and try all sorts of things to combat it. My high school had a different approach — one that definitely helped shape my philosophies outlined in this book. We were allowed to SKIP FINALS if we had less than two absences in the 2nd semester and a C average or better. POSITIVE REINFORCEMENT that supported the school's goals (kids in school, getting good grades) and the student's goals (no finals!). It is strongly recommended that schools re-implement this program for its students – and you use this analogy as a basis for your new management philosophy.

ATTENDANCE RECORD

REPORT CARD
Algebra — C
Chemistry — B
English — A
History — B
Spanish — B
B

Today's schools should instill this philosophy versus the heavy-handed approach so prevalent today. Get it? Giving us what *we* wanted (no finals), got the school what *they* wanted (our butts in their classroom every day). The negative reinforcement in our society and business doesn't work! How many approaches have you seen that try to battle obesity, smoking/drinking, etc? We all know we're not *supposed* to do those things, but do we? A little of the "Send Flowers to the Living" philosophy will work in these areas as well. Focus and reward the positive things to ensure we get more of it.

Before we proceed, I challenge you on something I saw demonstrated by "Mr. POS", Rich Wilkins (**rich@mrpos.com** or 858.566.0320) at a conference:

What do you see inside the box below?

At this point, you probably just said "a black dot." Over 99.9% of this box is WHITE, yet most people (especially managers) focus on the .1% imperfection (and waste valuable time and effort to change it). How do your employees react when all you do is harp on the negative? Do you buy flowers only when you did something wrong?

Do you spend the majority of your time:

- Focusing on what is going right or wrong?
- With your best people or worst people?
- Investing your money in high yield (good) investments or low yield (bad) investments?

Are you one of the top performers in your company?

- Does your boss spend a lot of time with you?
- Do you like working on things you are good at or being forced to do things you do not really like?
- Do you think you would excel with a little more recognition, which included spending time with your boss and/or the 'top brass' or experts in your company?

As you know, it is really difficult to change people. Stop trying to force them to be something they'll never become. Instead, explore what their strengths are and put them in a position to leverage those skills for the benefit of the organization and themselves. Therefore, spend the majority of your time with the talented employees. As you will see later in the book, the group of people you have that perform on occasion can also be your ally. To maximize their effectiveness, you need to discover why they only perform in certain conditions or situations and ensure those conditions are met more frequently. Finally, minimize the time spent with those who have little talent – chances are you will be replacing them anyway. For example, I have no vertical leaping ability. You could hire the best coach in the world and train me for hours on end, yet I'd never be able to dunk a basketball. Why waste the coach's time teaching me that skill? Have him/her spend time with people that can dunk or find another skill such as rebounding or defense that will allow me to help the team in a more effective manner.

Your best performers will do even more if you reward and recognize their contributions. They are left alone and often taken for granted. Show them new and improved ways to do things. Offer learning opportunities for them and listen to their input. It will provide a great return for you and your company. Since your time is limited, working with this group is far more beneficial to yourself and your company. The returns will pay off far quicker. If you had the choice to invest at a 10% return or a 2% return, you would obviously pick the 10% return. Why? In the long run, it nets you more money. Use the same approach with your people.

Where do bosses put their best sales people or managers: in the best territories/departments or the worst? Typically, they're placed in the worst (to fix them). What is the upside in that market versus the best ones? Put the 'aces in their places.' The great manager or salesperson can have a bigger impact on the company by being placed in the top areas or departments. The same process should be applied to your employees, yet most managers spend time with those who under-perform. You would not keep putting money in the 2% investment would you?

If you are still having trouble grasping the concept, think about sports teams. Who gets the ball most often? When it's a close game, the best player gets the opportunity. Do they miss sometimes? Sure. But the highest chance of success is with that person. Approach your team the same way – give the best people the chance to make you the most money.

Will you have to pay more (or recognize them frequently)? Yes. But it's worth it. After all, how well did the Chicago Bulls do once Michael Jordan retired? Not only did they suffer the loss of one of the all-time greats, they haven't been able to recruit the talent to make them a winning team. Losing the best performers not only hurts your chances in business today, it also damages the ability to attract the best for the future.

In even simpler terms, think about your strengths and weaknesses. If you can't dance, play music at all or play a particular sport, the best teachers in the world may never be able to teach you to do these things well. Why waste their time on someone who doesn't have the potential? Let them spend time with those with the talent. After all, whom would you want to coach: the world's #1 golfer or a struggling pro? Starting to see the picture?

So, let us dive in. You will not only learn to create a recognition culture in your organization but how to unleash the power of your team and see them (and yourself) rewarded for achieving the missions and goals of your organization.

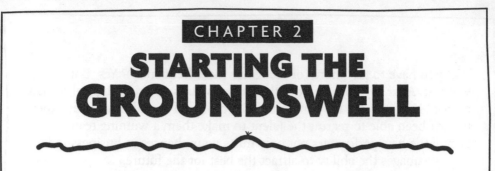

STARTING THE GROUNDSWELL

WHICH CAME FIRST, PERFORMANCE OR MORALE?

Much like the chicken and egg argument, the question can be debated for hours on end. However, this particular question has a definite answer: a simple one that most managers may not know. Often those in supervisory roles try to be friends with their employees to keep them happy. Softball teams, employee parties and the like are nice, but they don't ensure success in the company/ department/restaurant/store. It's like giving out trophies to *all* the teams in a sports league when we're young – performance is not aligned with getting a reward. Tie the fun and rewards to company, group and individual performance. You need to recognize performance to ensure it is repeated!

Karl Malone, one of the top professional basketball players of all time, recently made a statement that illustrates the importance of understanding this point. He said, "I don't want to be on a team where there is no opportunity to win, where there are players playing just to get a paycheck." How many employees does your company have that are just "playing to get a paycheck?" A colleague and former boss, Woody Berry, asked this question of all new managers with the company. He was taught this same principle 20 years ago during his days with Steak and Ale – again, not a new premise, but one that, to this day is still NOT practiced by your competition.

Ask your team this simple question:

Does Performance drive Morale or does Morale drive Performance?

If your group is like most, the majority (if not all) will say that morale drives performance. Now, ask them to explain *HOW* morale drives performance, without using performance terms in their answers. Here is what they'll probably say:

- When people do a good job, their manager says "thanks". (Performance 1st)

- When everyone pitches in, they feel good (Performance 1st)

- It's fun to work in a place that's busy (Performance 1st)

Others may say the following, but these don't ensure performance:

- We have a softball team and play other stores/departments.

- We have monthly parties and it's fun to work here.

- Oh good, _____ is managing today (The country club is open!).

- Our company/department has the best flag football team in the league.

Although all these points are valid and have some merit within the organization, none lead to performance. Just look at various sports teams – every league has them – they could pay high salaries and have the best fringe benefits, but players don't want to go there until they WIN! Winning organizations have people waiting to join them! Athletes will often take less money just to win that coveted championship. Creating that type of atmosphere will set you apart in today's tough job market.

A comprehensive benefit package and competitive pay will get employees in the door. To keep them, however, the company needs to be winning within the industry. How often do you see a "Now Hiring" ad for Outback Steakhouse, Southwest Airlines, The Container Store, Chick-Fil-A or many of the most respected companies in the country? If you do, typically it is only because they are growing or expanding into a new market. With management turnover in the single digits, do you think it's because of the "fluff" in those organizations? Hardly. These groups are winning in their respective industries and, guess what? Their people are happy and staying. Furthermore, these companies are the most respected from a service/guest standpoint as well.

Potential employees come to you most often because they think you are a winning organization. Once they see what the managers are made of, they decide if they are going to stay. Managers need to drive performance and winning in the three key areas – sales, people and profits. Satisfaction and great morale will follow. I challenge you to show me a happy organization that is losing (not applicable to the fans of the Chicago Cubs and Boston Red Sox)!

GUEST / CUSTOMER / CLIENT LOYALTY

A marketing approach to people management

Marketing is all about impressions. Get your target demographic to see your brand as many times in as many places as possible. Eventually they will purchase. Not every consumer, but enough to provide a financial return to the company. If it's a quality product or experience, the guest will continue to buy it and create long-term value for the business. The same approach will work with employees, yet it's commonly overlooked. Recognizing performance will create impressions with your employees to build their loyalty.

If you look at much of today's marketing focus, it utilizes rewards to create brand loyalty. Airlines, hotels, grocery stores, rental car companies, etc. all have some sort of Frequent Shopper/Flier program. What approach are they taking? Simple: they reward those who perform for that company (i.e. spend lots of dollars)! Does it cost money? Sure, but it's a very focused method to drive business and create loyalty. It has been shown that purchasing increases as loyalty does. Take this same approach with your people! The people that do the most get the most (i.e. loyal employees will provide the greatest return). Reward them for it!

I tend to be loyal to one rental-car company. Why? Because they reward me with free stuff – things their competition does not offer, and things I want. I rent approximately sixty cars per year and had rented with one of the top rental car agencies for years. When one of the other rental car companies started a frequent renter program (where you accumulated points to save towards golf or ski equipment and free vacations), guess what? I switched and earned enough points to outfit my entire family with new golf clubs and equipment! For those that don't play golf, they also offer ski equipment, sunglasses and frequent-flier miles.

Did it cost them? About $2,000 in prizes: However, I spent over $25,000 with them *and* their competitor lost $25,000 in sales – a double bonus! The challenge you have is to do the same thing with your employees – reward the frequent performer! The basic needs the rental car company provides (types of cars, price, availability, service) are similar to all the others. The only difference is the way they appreciate their frequent renters – coupons for future rentals and a point system to allow the purchase of various items. Using this system as an employer is simple: provide the basic needs (competitive compensation and benefits) and then reward the employees who provide the greatest return to the organization.

Airlines have realized for a long time that the frequent business flier is their bread and butter – generating a very large portion of their profits. If someone is a frequent flier, do they prefer the elevated-status treatment they receive versus being treated like all the other fliers, regardless of the amount they fly? Certainly they do. If someone is an infrequent traveler, which do they prefer? They prefer the airline that treats everyone the same, of course.

Most frequent travelers like the special treatment they receive due to the large amount of business they provide to an airline. It is nice to be rewarded with extra perks for providing the airline so much business. Will some people get offended? Maybe. But, if the airline has to have someone be dissatisfied, they would obviously prefer the infrequent flier on the discount fare versus the frequent full-fare business traveler. Besides, those infrequent fliers have a couple of options: they could fly more often to obtain that status, or fly another airline (and still be treated the same way if they are not a frequent flier on that airline).

How can leaders use that approach with their employees? Simple – create the same loyalty by providing the perks and recognition to the people who perform the best – they make the biggest impact on the company. People tend to be loyal to things, causes and companies they believe in – utilize that to your advantage. Like the airlines, will some people disagree with the system? Yes. But would you rather lose the frequent performer or one who rarely performs? In addition, those employees who perform only under certain conditions will choose to 'get off the fence' and step up to the elevated status. If you want fairness, be fair to those who do perform and let the non-performers go work for another company!

EMPLOYEE LOYALTY

Take the *exact same* marketing/business approach with your employees. Treat your top people the best – not the worst (i.e. ignoring them). Think about how you go out of your way to get those frequent flier/shopper/hotel guest points – often times you spend more money just to earn those points (think about the interest you pay on that credit card balance just to earn more airline miles). Chance are, you are already practicing this strategy *for yourself* – now implement it for your employees! Create that same feeling within your employees – have them go out of their way (above and beyond) to earn those same perks. Your job as a manager/owner/operator is to create employee loyalty within your organization. The employees that **do** the most should **receive** the most.

Will it cost you? Yes. But far less than having to hire and train replacements if they leave. Create an environment where they stay with you because of all the things you do for them. We've all seen studies of how much it costs to lose an employee – often 2-3 times their salary, yet many companies still lose people over a fraction of that cost (tripping over dollars to pick up pennies).

If you still disagree with this principle, retake the simple test in chapter 1!

●

What do you see? If you see a white box, proceed to the next chapter. If you still focus on that black dot, review the principles covered so far and move into the mindset of "Sending Flowers to the Living ".

A former boss of mine, Terry Spaight, often said, "Accountability is how often you bring something up." If you want people to do specific tasks, talk about them often. In most cases, managers talk about those 'black dots.' Managers fail, however, to hold their employees accountable to the things they do right. If you want your team to repeat good behaviors, you need to recognize them and talk frequently about them – no different than trying to stop the incorrect behaviors!

This proven management philosophy is the springboard for the rest of the book. Create winning teams and leverage the power of that team by rewarding your performers. Don't reward people "just for playing." Many managers try this strategy and 'fake' their sincerity. Employees see right through it. While you think employees may not be as smart as managers, why don't you try living on minimum wage (or close to it)!

ARE YOU WATERING THE RIGHT FLOWERS?

WHAT PLANET ARE YOU FROM?

If you can get your managers to focus on what the *employees want* versus *what you think they want,* you will outpace the competition. Your brand identity as an employer will create applicant inflow, while stopping good employee outflow. Many studies have been done over the years (most recently validated by renowned recognition expert, Bob Nelson) and they all seem to echo the same sentiment.

Managers think money is the primary motivator that employees want, while they feel being appreciated and 'in on things' are not. In fact, managers have ranked these two items as the least important to the employee. Employees, on the other hand, ranked these two items as the most important. They want to be a part of an organization that succeeds and recognizes the employees who provided that success. Money is important to them, but not as much as the other factors.

If managers think this way, they'll act this way. Why do people leave? Employees want to be appreciated first and foremost, yet managers do not grasp its importance. When the manager and employee are on different wavelengths, true success cannot be achieved. Maybe it is because management's focus is not aligned with the employees! Your business goals cannot be accomplished if the mind-set of your managers and employees are this far apart. All three parts of the wheel must be in balance.

MANAGE THE MIRROR

You have probably heard the expression, "Be careful when you point the finger at someone because three of those fingers are pointing at yourself!" Too often, we tend to blame others for our shortcomings or do not take ownership of our actions. Often times you hear, "I'd change it if I was the boss." Yeah, right! The challenge is to stop the revolving door! People tend to manage the way they get managed. Therefore, the common practice is, "I am not recognized by my boss, so I do not recognize my people."

It's not done purposely – most managers are totally unaware of how necessary and important a tool it can be for them.

Instead of complaining about your situation, look in the mirror and figure out how you can make it better. The answer is not softball teams and office parties – unless the party and team is a celebration for a business success. Sure, you are not in charge of everyone, but you are in charge of someone (yourself, at least). You can stop this practice by giving recognition to your people (in spite of what your company culture may be), and begin to train your boss. It appalls me to hear people complain about not getting recognized. If you wait for things to happen to you, they never will. Go out and get the recognition you want and need - and then recognize your people.

Ask leading questions of your boss and peers when you and your team have done something great. Pass that recognition onto your team. For those of you with workaholic bosses, leave them a voice mail real early/late so you give the appearance your working a little bit harder. In my experience, a person's 'skip-level' boss (two levels up) is critical in their development. Since they do not spend as much time with that person (and they hold the keys to their career), help them by passing feedback up to your boss so you can pass it down to your employees. A few examples to generate some recognition from your boss:

"What did you think of the sales/profit from the department last week?"

"How did you like that presentation?"

"Have you seen what _____ in the department did?"

"How did you like that idea?"

"What did ____ say about that new system we implemented?"

"What else do we need to do to help you move up/make your job easier?"

The basis of this philosophy is for managers to reward people who perform. Remember, #1 on the employees' list is appreciation for the work they are doing. When employees perform, it must be recognized by the managers. The more someone performs, the greater the recognition. Otherwise, the employee will not feel appreciated for their efforts and will look elsewhere. (especially if they are putting forth the extra effort.) If your employees are getting that recognition, you will be winning, achieving your goals and, ultimately, creating a great place to work.

Later in the book you will see contests and incentive systems that can help you jumpstart the process and ensure your reward and recognition system revolves around driving the sales and profits of the business. Everyone has had jobs (and probably left them) where they did not feel fully appreciated for their contributions, or where they felt left out. Rewarding your star performers will make them feel "in" and appreciated for what they do – taking care of your guests/clients/customers and creating a loyal following!

Now that you know what employees want from their job and employer (and you know what you need to focus on to manage them), it is time to look at specific examples of how you can address your employees' top wants (appreciation/recognition for their performance).

Since you have made it this far into the book, you must be interested in the subject matter. To be effective, you will need to become more than 'interested' and turn these ideas into action. As Jim Sullivan reminds audiences during his seminars: the belief has to match the behavior. You may believe you need to lose weight, but your behavior is eating too many donuts. Will you ever accomplish your goal? In this case, you believe recognition is important, but what do your actions say? Commit to making the cultural shift within your organization and do not accept excuses or anything less. Start with your own behavior and train your boss. The momentum will be generated in the right direction. Since people cannot argue with results (especially those achieved the right way), others will begin coming to you for advice and suggestions.

PUTTING THOUGHTS INTO ACTION

 "Thanks" – even for minor things such as coming in on time, doing the basics, coming in proper uniform, getting the memo out on time, the package arriving on time or doing what they promised. Handwritten thank you notes attached to their paychecks go a long way. Do you think your competition is doing this? While thanking people takes time and 'time is money,' you can afford the time to say 'thanks.'

 Listening – to their thoughts and suggestions. People really thrive on seeing their ideas put into action. Who knows better what your guests or clients want than your front line employees? Your kitchen/warehouse/ distribution/office staff also will have great ideas to increase efficiency in the "back" of the house. Your sales staff knows what your clients want.

Delivery drivers, administrative assistants, etc. know what will make their job easier. Listen and reward them. There's an old expression, "the farther up the ladder, the less you know about how to use the copier!" Listen and learn from those who are doing the job everyday – they are the key-holders to everyday improvement. Be available for your people.

 Communicating – Let the team know what is going on within the company/department/unit by using newsletters, e-mails, pre-shift or daily 'huddles' or meetings. Provide updates, post items you are tracking (i.e. sales goals, costs), post guest letters or comment cards on the company intranet or internal web page - it is a great way to give recognition so the company can see how their star performers are doing. Football players huddle after nearly every play - do you?

 Tools – Have them available so they can do their job. It's hard enough to do the job right, especially if all the tools are not available or being used.

 Reviews – Give formal performance reviews on time. More importantly, hold "informal" reviews on a frequent basis. Let your employees know how they are doing every one to two weeks – review items such as attendance, sales results, budgets, cost saving ideas, etc.

Schedule – While many managers expect their staff to work countless hours, they rarely respect the staff's time. Allow flexibility when employees need it. They will be recharged and perform when you need it. If you have hourly-type positions, make sure schedules are posted on time and honor employee requests whenever possible. If we expect employees to be here on time, their schedule should be up when we say it will. How many times have you worked for someone who expected this type of behavior, yet never exhibited it? They had a separate set of rules, right? Therefore,

 Lead by Example – Model the behavior you want from your employees.

These things all seem simple, yet they are the difference between great managers and the good managers. *Make these suggestions common practice.*

A few tips gathered over the years to help move you in this direction:

1) **REMINDER "TRIGGER"** – Whether it's a note in your day planner, PDA or an alert that pops up on your PC, set up a system to help remind yourself to praise and recognize your people. I've even heard of people putting coins in one pocket and each time they pay a compliment, they move one coin to the other pocket. Find a system that works for you and use it!

2) **FOCUS ON THE POSITIVE** – Try this strategy the next time you have an employee issue: Instead of ripping into the employee who comes in late, reward every employee who came in on time that day with a 'thank you' or a free fifteen-minute time pass. Do it in a public fashion so the employee that came in late can see it. The late employee will get the message very quickly. It makes an incredible statement to the employees who come in late and, more importantly, recognizes all the employees who made it to work on time. When was the last time someone showed their appreciation for you arriving on time?

3) **80/20 RULE** – Try to say four positive things to your employees for every one negative comment. Most managers have it the other way around. Many people are not comfortable receiving praise (it embarrasses them). Some have never received praise from prior bosses and therefore have become a product of their environment. STOP the revolving door of negativity.

4) **SANDWICH PHILOSOPHY** – When you do have to give some negative feedback sandwich it between two positives. Occasionally, you may have a lot of negative (a 'double meat' sandwich), but you still need to sandwich the positives around it.

How would the average manager handle a situation where an employee comes in late?

TYPICAL MANAGER COMMENTS

"Thanks for gracing us with your presence today!"
"Glad you could FINALLY make it."
"I didn't know your schedule said, 10:13, I thought it said 10:00."
"Get to work, you're late!"
"Where have you been?"

"SANDWICH" MANAGER

"John, normally you are my best employee and it's critical you are here on time so you can do that awesome job of guest service. Get out there and make it happen."

5) **"AND", not "BUT"** – Notice in the above example how the manager used the word "AND" as they moved from the positive to the negative feedback. All too often, managers say something positive and then use the word "BUT". The minute the employee hears that, it discounts everything that was said prior to it (all the positive stuff). For example,

"John, normally you're my best employee, BUT…"

"I know, BUT…"

"Well, sure, BUT…"

"Yes, BUT…"

Once they hear the word "BUT," they have just forgotten anything you've said before that. I'd also encourage you to try this strategy at home with your spouse and children.

6) **PRACTICE PRAISING YOURSELF AND YOUR BOSS**– Everyone needs more positive reinforcement. If you happen to work for a boss who does not provide enough positive feedback, or who does not practice the items outlined above, chances are you will lack the same skills. You need the positive feedback, so give some to yourself – whether in the mirror, to yourself mentally, in your car - practice. It is very uncomfortable to give praise if you're unaccustomed to it. Do not forget to prompt your boss. You will be able to hear different styles of praising and recognition, so when the opportunity to praise an employee arises, it will flow naturally.

BRIBERY OR RECOGNITION?

Many people ask during or after my seminars, "Why do we have to give more for what we already pay them to do? That's bribery!" Again, most managers are of the baby boomer generation where the attitude of lifelong employment and 'do it because it is the right thing to do' prevail. However, this is not how our employees were raised. They crave the limelight and demand that extra attention. Use that to your advantage! Before we move on, let's look at the definition of the two terms:

BRIBERY: *A payment in advance of anticipating something in return.* For example, you pay off someone hoping to get something in return. Examples include paying ransom in hopes of a hostage's return or a payoff to someone in hopes of them getting you favorable treatment.

RECOGNITION: *'A little something extra'* **in return** for having done something well.

Recognition is delivered after the performance. They have already completed what you want and you are recognizing them. While it is definitely something extra (above pay and benefits), it is NOT bribery.

Therefore, *SALARY IS BRIBERY.* After all, you pay someone in anticipation of them doing the job you pay them to do. Like bribery, they get something (a paycheck and benefits), but do not necessarily have to perform (if the manager accepts that inferior level of performance). Recognition, on the other hand is delivered after the performance has been completed.

Think about sports. The big contract is recognition for a job well done. The superstars continue that level of performance during the next contract period. Others, however, tend only to perform during 'contract years.' They land the big deal based on their one good year. Once they do, they slack off. These are not stars; they are 'fence-sitters' or 'blinking stars' – sporadic performers no different than an employee in a restaurant who asks 'who is closing tonight?' If the manager with high standards is on duty, they perform at a high level. If the manager with low standards is working, they perform at a lower level – similar to playing at the level of your competition. They perform when they want to, depending on the situation. One could argue their salary is bribery – they are being guaranteed a specific amount, but the owner is not guaranteed performance in return.

Now that you have some basic ideas of how to create a recognition culture, let's take it one step further so you can fully understand the principles behind spending time with your star performers.

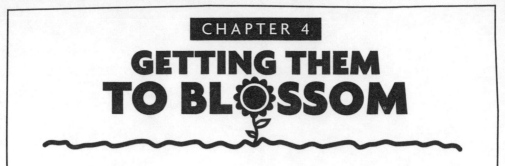

GETTING THEM TO BLOSSOM

Confucius once said, "Only the wisest and stupidest of men never change." I agree with him with one caveat. While these groups will not change their performance, the wise people will change *companies!* If performers do not get treated right, they are smart enough to know to look for a place that suits them better. We all know the 'stupidest' ones will not change their habits or their companies (we have to do that for them).

If your company is not already recognizing the stars, you will want to implement these changes soon. Very few companies are practicing this philosophy and it will set you apart. Today's managers often ignore their stars since they are accustomed to their high level of performance. Hopefully, your competition manages that way because the stars of today can take their show anywhere – anywhere, that is, where they will be appreciated!

While sitting in the dentist's chair one day, I saw a funny sign that can be applied here as well. It said, "You don't need to floss ALL your teeth, only the ones you want to keep!" Obviously we need to keep all our teeth. Tweak that a little for your employees:

> *You don't need to recognize all your employees,*
> *only the ones you want to keep!*

You will definitely want to keep the top-performers, as well as those that have the talent, but may not always use it. Those who perform on occasion need to be recognized when they are doing a great job so they will be enticed to repeat those behaviors more often. The non-performers, those who do not have the talent or who choose to be negative about everything the company does, need to be encouraged to look elsewhere for employment!

OVERVIEW

Any time a manager tries to change something or implement a new program/procedure, the employees will fall into one of three distinct groups – '**Make it happen**' people, '**Watch it happen**' people and '**Wonder what happened**' people or, as they are dubbed here:

"Shining Stars", "Blinking Stars" and **Anchors.** How you manage will determine which group leaves.

Managers tend to ignore their superstars. Confucius said the wisest never change, so why not leave well enough alone (don't forget about the accountability definition)? The blinking stars demonstrate the talent, but only when they want to. They are not committed to it fully yet. What can we do so we ensure they perform a greater percentage of the time? They perform while someone is looking over their shoulder, so why can't they do it when nobody is watching? The last group, the anchors, were most likely a bad hire. While not bad people, they are just in the wrong environment or position. Maybe a change of scenery will help them. They will not change no matter how much anyone else wants them to. They are committed to being who they are!

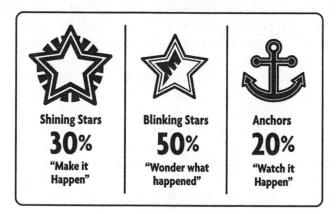

Shining Stars	Blinking Stars	Anchors
30%	**50%**	**20%**
"Make it Happen"	"Wonder what happened"	"Watch it Happen"

MAKE IT HAPPEN (Shining Stars)

This select group does whatever you say – They are the PERFORMERS. They are described as 'the top 20% who generate 80% of the profits/sales/work'.

WATCH IT HAPPEN (Blinking Stars)

Waiting to see what happens. Some days they perform great, while other days they do not. It is the star athlete who only performs during a contract year or someone whose performance depends on who is around, the weather or their boss that day. Some typical comments you might hear from this group would be:

"Must be the program-du-jour."

"He's always like this after a seminar, don't worry, it'll go away."

WONDER WHAT HAPPENED (Anchors)

These old dogs are not learning any new tricks! Anchors drag down or at least slow down the team. Can you afford to have too many of them in the water? No matter how hard the rest of the team is working, the team cannot perform at its highest level when this group is dragging them down.

"This is so stupid, I'm not doing it."

"I'm not suggestive selling – it's on the menu – they can read"

"I don't do this when _____ is here, so why should I for you?"

ANOTHER VIEW

To quote Terry Spaight again, he used a similar method to explain it another way. He says, "30% of your employees will never steal from you, while 20% will always steal from you. The other 50% will do whatever the manager allows." If you have loose controls, the middle group will steal from you. If you have tight controls, they will not. Therefore, by having tight controls, you'll have at least 80% of the people *not stealing* from you. The 20% is always going to steal from you, so at least ensure that 80% aren't! Yet most managers today will create all types of rules systems and processes to try and deter the 20% from stealing. They create elaborate systems while overlooking the basics. You will then have 70% of the people stealing from you! Instead of that group not stealing, it creates all kinds of obstructions for the stars to do their work efficiently and they get frustrated.

THE INDIVIDUAL

Take yourself for example. What areas are your major strengths? Major opportunities? Traits that are average? If you take an overview of your skills, some obviously standout as strengths, while others are glaring weaknesses. Many, however, are in the middle – they are neither strengths nor weaknesses.

The smart person will spend a majority of their time maximizing strengths, a lesser portion trying to develop the skills that are just 'average' and managing around weaknesses by surrounding themselves with people talented in those areas. If we spent all our time trying to 'fix' our weaknesses, we would never succeed and our strengths would fade away. Do you manage each person in your group that way – focusing on their strengths? Collectively as a group, where are you spending *your* time?

Which group does the typical manager spend their time with? Let's see...

SCENARIO – NEW SELLING PROGRAM IMPLEMENTATION

You just read this book and implemented a new selling strategy in your company. As usual with all new things, your employees fall into the three main groups outlined previously. What does each of the three do?

Shining Stars – They realize they will make bigger bonus/tips and jump all over it. They are happy!

Blinking Stars – Wait and see – really not doing anything different.

Anchors – Complain endlessly about how stupid this new program is!

The program is going OK (mainly due to the Shining Stars performance), but not really catching on like we had hoped. Here are two typical scenarios:

MANAGER #1 – We'll call him "Majority Man!"

He does what most of today's managers do – spends his time with the 20% (The Anchors). He is trying to get them to quit complaining about these new expectations and goals. What happens? The Blinking Stars become Anchors! As you know, employees will do what gets the manager's attention – in this case, moan and gripe!

RESULTS

With the focus on the "Anchors," the "Shining Stars" leave.

What do you have? 70% of the people doing the *exact opposite* of what you wanted! How about those Shining Stars? Tired of working for a place that allows its managers to console the non-performers, they move on down the road to the next company. Are they hard to replace? You bet! They also take with them the value they provide to your competitor! Big, double-whammy! This is an unfortunate scenario that plays out everyday all across America!

MANAGER #2 – "SEND FLOWERS" Manager

She has already read this book and knows exactly what to do – she spends all her time rewarding the Shining Stars when they perform! Her words of thanks and appreciation catch the eye of the Blinking Stars. What do they do? They realize the benefit of performing and start mimicking the behaviors exhibited by the Shining Stars. What do you have?

RESULTS

With the focus on the "Shining Stars," the "Anchors" leave.

You have 80% of the people doing *exactly* what you want. What happens to the anchors? They get tired of working in a 'stupid place like this one' and leave. Are they hard to replace? Not really. Hopefully, they go to your competitors! You can now hire in some winners that will thrive in a culture such as this and have everyone paddling in the same direction. Guess what – this 'stupid' place is building sales and growing profits.

AVERAGING UP

By adopting this strategy, you can also aid in your recruiting efforts. Not only will you have a greater story to attract candidates, but you will also be able to **"Average-up"** your team. Averaging up simply means that every person you hire is better than the one they are replacing. If you practice the "Majority Man" philosophy, it is virtually impossible to average up – in fact, the exact opposite happens. How can you continue to 'average up' when you are losing your best people? If you are spending time with the performers and your anchors are leaving, averaging up is simple, as you are always replacing the worst performers!

When the non-performers are leaving, each person you hire has a great chance of being superior to the one you just lost. Therefore, the average performance of your team will increase and the environment everyone works in will be entirely different as you are weeding out the 'bad apples.'

For whatever reason, today's managers are much more like "Majority Man" and create "Churnover" of epic proportions in many industries. Don't hear me wrong; this style will not eliminate turnover - it will *cause good turnover* (but at a lower rate than the turnover experienced in the industry today). The challenge is to try this simple exercise with your staff. The next time you have a change, focus on the positive (see the 99.9% white box) with your employees and see what happens. Guaranteed great results.

Imagine how many fewer cutbacks a company would have during an economic downturn. Mass layoffs send out the good with the bad. By focusing on rewarding performance, you enable your company to continually replace the non-performers. It is not only a positive message to those doing the job well, but prevents a company from getting rid of the top employees when times are tight. You find the stars keep on performing and, yes it is O.K. to reward them. The Blinking Stars increase in performance will be the part that pays for any incentive plan you enact. You can then eliminate the anchors. After all, anchors keep you in one place and unable to move forward!

CHAPTER 5
THE WRONG FERTILIZER

Nearly all studies regarding recognition today agree on one thing – Money is not the answer! While competitive base salaries or wages are necessary to attract applicants to the company, you find that it is not always what people want when it comes to recognition. This may be contrary to the "American Way" and slogans such as:

"Money isn't everything, but fork some over and watch me smile."

"Money can't buy you love, but it can rent a good imitation."

"Money isn't everything, but rich is better."

"Money doesn't suck."

IS IT THE BENJAMINS?

Perhaps the most telling statistic and argument on this point you can find are today's servers/salespeople/managers that work for cash tips or sales bonuses. If money were an effective motivator, servers would *always* suggest additional items. Employees on a bonus plan would *always* be driving sales. After all, they receive between 15% and 20% of the total sale as a tip or a commission (portion of the proceeds) on their sales. They control their own income.

How many of us get that opportunity? Go home today and tell your spouse, "I could have made more money today, but I just didn't feel like it." Why wouldn't they suggest that $4.95 appetizer which earns them an additional $0.75 in tips per table (and earns a restaurant $4.95 in sales), try to sell the matching sweater, get a guest to sign up for the extended warranty or sell the client up to the next price break? Seems like an automatic thing to do, but it illustrates that money does not work as a great form of driving performance. It is part of compensation and does need to be competitive. It is not a great form of recognition or incentive.

Think back to when you were growing up. All the awards you were given; what were they? They were always trophies, plaques, medals and certificates. Many of us still have them tucked away for safekeeping. Did grandma or another relative always slip you a little cash? Yes? Do you remember what you did with it? I didn't think so. Cash as a reward has no staying power or 'trophy value'. A few tips on cash:

- **Cash (including bonuses) is considered part of salary.**

- **Can't brag to others about it.**

- **Often no 'intangible' recognition.**

Most of us use cash (whether it is salary or bonus/tips) to pay bills or debt. Often, we cannot remember what we did with the money. People simply consider bonuses as part of their basic compensation package and often expect them. These days, the bonus 'check' is not even a check – simply a copy of a deposit that was directly sent into your bank account. In the old days, the boss had to deliver the checks and had an opportunity to show their appreciation. Many people do not even feel bonuses affect their performance, as many of the factors are out of their control. What do we do with our basic compensation? Pay bills and living expenses.

AN EXPENSIVE PROPOSITION

Not only does cash NOT improve performance, it is used on items no differently than a paycheck. The purpose of an incentive program is to reward employees for a job well done, and to bond them with the company – cash does not do it. It simply gets lumped into their "salary." Additionally, there's no daily reminder of the reward (i.e. like looking at a specific reward such as a plaque or gift bought with a gift certificate). The final nail in the coffin is the "ego test." People typically do not discuss money (i.e. a cash award), unless they find it lacking. You run the risk of undervaluing their contribution.

Chapter 6 will cover a long list of awesome awards that will excite your employees to perform at levels not previously seen in your organization. Best of all, it will cost you less than you (or they) think!

THE EXCEPTION

A few notes on cash: people do need (and like) money. It is just not the best long-term form of recognition. A good tip from Jim Sullivan illustrates a way to create some trophy value with cash:

Instead of giving someone a $20 bill as a thank you, give them ten $2 bills or twenty of the new $1 coins. While people still may use them as cash (i.e. to buy gas), these items will generate the question, "Where did these come from?" The answer? You! They are unique and people will ask them where they got them when they go to use them.

Many other people will simply save these unique items. They will constantly be reminded of you, your company and the recognition of their performance.

CHAPTER 6

THE RIGHT FERTILIZERS

"Send Flowers to the Living" is all about rewarding your performers and turning the Blinking Stars into Shining Stars. If cash is not the answer, what is? Salary and tips/bonus cover the *needs*; recognition covers those things you *want* (but may not be able to afford in lieu of basic necessities). The most important result is you will remember it – it has trophy value. At a previous job, I received a gift certificate to buy new golf clubs on my 15-year anniversary. Had I received a check for $500, I would have spent it and forgotten about it. I still use those clubs and remember who gave them to me. The problem? Most of us have to wait for our anniversaries to receive that recognition. While those milestones are impressive and need to be celebrated, not many people make it to those milestones these days. Celebrate performance in the interim.

Over the last five years, I have developed and overseen plenty of contests – ones that reward anyone from young, part-time employees to the most seasoned of managers. Take the advice here and avoid some of the pitfalls that have been made in the past. Later, we will discuss the different types of contests - this section will focus on the types of rewards that drive performance in your organization.

Whether it is a contest you design or starting to reward and appreciate people for their contributions, do not forget about the personal side of the recognition. While it is great to receive tangible things for performance, how it is presented can make all the difference in the world. A manager, co-worker or boss taking time to thank someone is what is truly important in making an employee feel appreciated. Everyone has received some type of award over the years. The award simply serves as a reminder of how you felt at the time it was presented. The memory of the presentation, small or large, is where the value lies.

As today's world becomes more automated and technology-driven, it is easy to send an electronic card to someone and include an online gift certificate with it – whether it's to reward performance or send as an anniversary or birthday gift. It is better than no recognition, but is it really personal? Are you truly making the employee feel appreciated? How much thought and effort truly went into that present/reward? It's the delivery that matters!

WHAT TO REWARD

How often has a marketing department developed a great product only to see it fail at the operational level, or a new program be implemented by the corporate office yet the field managers and employees do not embrace it with the same passion? The old expression "marketing can bring them in once, but it is operations' job to bring them back" rings true. Especially for sales programs, marketing must convince the sellers, distributors and/or vendors what is in it for them if the program is to be a true success.

Taking a few dollars from the ad budget and applying it to rewarding top sales performers will aid in the sales of the product. All the money spent on snazzy ads, commercials and print advertising will be wasted if the salesperson does not fulfill their obligations. As mentioned earlier, if we want the frontline employees and sales force to drive sales and profitability, they need to be rewarded and appreciated for it – all three parts of the wheel need to be in sync.

Focusing on rewarding sales is simple because it is easily quantifiable. What about all those people not directly involved in sales? What opportunities do we have to recognize and reward them?

NON-SALES RECOGNITION OPPORTUNITIES

- Cost-saving ideas and behaviors
- Referral Bonuses / Bounties for New Hires
- Employee of the Moment
- Attendance and/or Timeliness
- Thanks for staying late or arriving early
- Covering a shift or project at the last minute
- Great Performance
- Hitting Profit Targets

- Surpassing productivity goals or targets
- Showing up on time
- Going above and beyond
- Great comments from guests or clients
- Simply doing their job consistently
- Memos or shipments done on time
- Assisting co-workers
- Special occasions in their lives – birthdays, anniversaries, etc.
- Setting records – productivity, safety, production time
- Covering for you or a co-worker
- Getting through a busy period or season
- Not making any mistakes on an order or memo
- Improving in an area you coached them on
- Performance improvement in an area they were deficient
- Learning new skills to help the company and themselves
- Doing things prior to being told
- Having a smile on their face or a great attitude
- Being a team player

Here is an extensive list of rewards that are effective. Rewards and recognition are personal – know what your employees' likes and dislikes are so the reward will have value to them. There will be a temptation to focus on the large rewards, but do not overlook the importance of building the trust within your employees by utilizing all the free and low-cost methods to recognize small contributions – like a daily dose of vitamins (inexpensive and beneficial, but often overlooked).

MOTIVATING REWARDS

Many people get scared away by the "sticker shock" of paying for the awards. Chapter 7 will provide a list of tips to ensure that the money you spend on these rewards pays itself back many times over.

$0 – $10 REWARDS

- 10 minutes of your time to listen
- "Thank you," "I appreciate it," "I'm sorry"
- Thank you notes (handwritten)
- Thank you e-mail (cc: the top brass and peers)
- Electronic thank you card
- Name a day or part of the business (office, warehouse, restaurant) after them
- Pass for a free car wash
- Movie pass
- 'Quick Pick' Lottery tickets - TIP: Don't use 'scratch-off' cards as they will scratch them off right there and get upset if they do not win – Jim Sullivan
- One video rental gift card
- Fast food gift certificate
- Free coffee gift card/certificate
- Bring in breakfast, donuts or coffee one morning
- Trade with other businesses – many are willing to trade their goods/services for yours. Your cost is significantly reduced since you are not paying their full face value (it really only costs you the cost of goods you traded them).
- Parking Spot close to entrance / front door
- Picture on the "Wall of Fame"
- Create a recognition wall of all the company milestones and records – safety, sales, cost containment, personal performances
- 15 or 30 minute Time Pass (Get out of Work Free)
- Ten cent raise = $4 per week for full-time employee (about $2 per week for part-time). A few of these over the course of a year versus waiting until the review presents numerous opportunities to say 'thanks' and recognize contributions

- Schedule flexibility (flex schedule, choice of days off, first choice on vacations)
- Peak day off
- First choice of schedules
- Additional Training for desired skills
- Hat, T-shirt or key-chain with your logo
- Vendor supplied items – hats, shirts, etc.
- Pins / buttons
- 30 minute phone card – International ones for those with family outside of the U.S.
- Free dinner / lunch for your employee's family
- Small bouquet of flowers
- Coffee mug

With all these awards, it is not the size or the dollar amount that matters. It simply is the boss saying 'thanks' and recognizing what someone does for the group. Much like a bonus check that is direct deposited, an e-mail that shows up with an online gift certificate can be viewed quite impersonally. Make sure it is personalized – announce it first, prior to the employee actually receiving the e-mail certificate.

$10 - $25 REWARDS

- CD / DVD / Video certificate
- Dry cleaning
- Movie rentals
- Gift certificates to local merchants – bookstores, hobby stores, clothing, online
- Four hour "Get Out of Work Free" Pass
- T-shirts, golf shirts with your logo
- Dinner for two at a casual restaurant
- Movie pass for two

- Gas cards

- 60 – 90 minute phone card

- Ten $2 bills

- Twenty gold $1 coins

- Magazine subscription (professional or their favorite hobby). Find out about your employees and this will personalize the reward. It maybe a magazine on their favorite sport or hobby, investing, computers, interests they have, etc. (keep it G-rated)! It will provide 12 months of reminders from you and the company.

- "*Super*-Certificates™" – Can be used online or offline and offers your choice of hundreds of original merchant gift certificates to choose from. Visit **www.GiftCertificates.com** for more information. They are available in various denominations.

$50 - $100+ REWARDS

- Upscale dinner for two

- Sports tickets

- Show tickets

- Eight hour "Get Out of Work Free" pass

- Round of golf

- Ski lift ticket

- Gift certificate to an electronics store

- One night hotel stay

- One day car rental certificate

- Electronic items

- Sweatshirts or jackets with a company logo

- Spa pass

- Clothing or home improvement certificate

- Mall certificate

- Larger denomination "*Super*-Certificates™" from **www.GiftCertificates.com**

AWARDS THAT DRIVE RESULTS

GIFT CARDS / CERTIFICATES – Provide a basic cash equivalent that allows the employees to get something for themselves (or others as gifts). The nice thing about gift cards is they let the employee choose what they want – you do not worry about making a mistake. Some of the most popular types are:

1) **RESTAURANTS** – Fast food certificates work great for lower-end rewards (book of five $1 certificates covers lunch for a day for them). Larger ones can be given ($10-$25 for casual dining restaurants or any local themed eatery you have nearby), or even high-end restaurants ($50 - $100) so your employees can take out that special someone (on you) to celebrate their achievements. Keeping their spouse or spousal equivalent happy will pay huge dividends for you. Many restaurants sell the certificates at a discount if you purchase large quantities, while chains that own multiple brands offer the flexibility to use their gift cards at all their concepts – more choices mean more value for less money!

2) **GAS CARDS** – All major chains offer these cards in values of $10 - $100. Filling up their tank is a great way to say "thanks." Does not have strong trophy value, but it ensures they do not "run out of gas" on the way in. These cards are ideal for teenagers, sales people, "soccer Moms" and college kids to help cover costs that Mom and Dad may not be helping with. And they'll remember who paid for that tank (or tanks) of gas each time they use the card.

3) **CD / ELECTRONIC STORES** – Music CD's, videos, DVD's and the equipment to play them on are extremely popular with employees of all ages. Cannot go wrong here.

4) **MALL CERTIFICATES** – Many shopping malls have gift certificates that are good at all their merchants in the mall. Lots of variety – every employee needs something from the mall.

5) **HOME IMPROVEMENT STORES**

6) **CLOTHING STORES**

7) **VIDEO STORES** – Sold in various increments. Can treat your employees to a night of movies and popcorn at home.

Some other great rewards to consider are:

VENDOR MERCHANDISE – Many of your suppliers will provide merchandise as prizes for your programs. They will provide hats, shirts, etc., if you are focusing on selling their products – low cost for you and some great stuff for your employees!

TIME OFF – Either a simple "Get out of work free" card – good for 15–30 minutes to arrive late or leave early (with manager approval) at lunch or the end of the day. You could even offer a paid day off on the high side. Simple things such as **schedule flexibility, flex-time or choice of hours costs you nothing**.

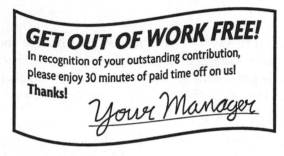

GET OUT OF WORK FREE!
In recognition of your outstanding contribution, please enjoy 30 minutes of paid time off on us!
Thanks!
Your Manager

MOVIE TICKETS/CERTIFICATES – A pass for two can save your employees $15 or more. Many larger movie chains offer a package for two for $25-30 that includes: two tickets, popcorn and two sodas. What a great gift, especially if combined with a dinner certificate and some paid time off.

PHONE CARDS –Much like gas cards, they help people offset some of the daily expenses in life. They work great for younger employees, people with kids in college or those with relatives overseas (international calling cards) you may employ. You can even get pre-paid cellular phones for your employees!

"UNIVERSAL" GIFT CARDS – These certificates are a unique type of gift with something for everyone interested in the outdoors. You can purchase five different types of "Universal" cards – Golf, Golf Lessons, Amusement Parks, Skiing or Snowboarding. The card is good at a large number of golf courses, amusement parks or ski resorts. Some require more than one card (i.e. a high-end golf course may be four cards to play, while the neighborhood course may be one). The same goes for the amusement parks and ski resorts. Golf cards and lessons work great for managers, sales reps, etc., while the others work great for the younger crowd. The upside? They are good all over the country at many places. The downside? You pay a slight premium for the cards over the normal price. Still, a great deal if paired with a paid day off. Visit **www.universaltickets.com** for more information.

CREDIT CARD COMPANIES – Many companies have come out with programs where recipients receive a personalized, pre-programmed stored value card good at any retailer accepting that type of credit card. It works just like a debit card - the set amount is automatically reduced after the purchases. Again, there is a nominal charge, but it is personalized with their name on the card and gives them great flexibility to use it wherever they choose.

TRAVEL CERTIFICATES – Depending on your budget, these are a great motivator for your manager-level employees. A free weekend trip can really get people performing at new levels. All major hotel chains, airline and rental car companies offer certificates that can be used to create a great escape for your top performers.

"E-CENTIVE" WEBSITES – You buy certificates of varying denominations and your employees can go online (or call) and choose from hundreds of different types of gift certificates – popular retailers, restaurants, hotels and airlines are all available. In seven to ten days the certificate of their choice is delivered to their home or, in the case of online merchants; the certificates are delivered instantly to their computer! UPSIDE: Virtually no management involvement from your side (or guess work as to which type of certificates to buy), and a LARGE number of choices. DOWNSIDE: Time to get awards to the employees if they do not have web access or you choose not to purchase the awards ahead of time and self-administer the program. Visit www.giftcertificates.com for more information.

GIFT CERTIFICATE CLEARINGHOUSES – There are many companies / websites that sell various certificates at face value or discounts. You can obtain certificates often at a discount and use them for your rewards.

INCENTIVE CATALOGS – There are numerous companies that will provide an all-encompassing catalog that includes a myriad of gifts and rewards at various prize levels. The benefits include no inventory for you to hold, a wide-range of merchandise and the costs are not incurred until later in the contest when the prizes are selected.

CHAPTER 6

It is highly recommended you include a personal, hand-written thank you note on Company letterhead to ensure the correlation between the item, their performance and your Company. The sincerity and presentation of the reward is what matters. For more information or specific companies, send me a note of what you are looking for to **tj@thepeoplepyramid.com.**

CHAPTER 7
USING CONTESTS TO DRIVE GROWTH

Everyone likes to win. Contests are an ideal way to unleash the company's competitive spirit and achieve your goals. They are most effective when used to drive sales of an item or product line, focus on key objectives or give your employees an extra incentive to break some records. These are a great catalyst to expedite the process of moving your company culture forward.

The little devil has popped on your shoulder and is now saying, "Yeah, but when the contest ends, everything goes back to the way it was!" Do not listen to that voice! While it is a natural first reaction, you will see that by giving constant rewards through your recognition tied to the contest, you will have reinforced the behaviors and they will generally remain above the pre-contest levels.

> Yeah, but when the contest ends, everything goes back to the way it was!

A large family-entertainment chain ran a suggestive selling contest rewarding their cashiers for selling extra cheese on pizzas, collector's cups and value packages. The contest rewarded the cashiers who sold over the historic levels of the company average. If you have the data and are in more of an individualized sales department, you can also design the contest to reward employees who sell over their own past historical levels (versus using the company averages). They received lottery-style cards that contained various point values and instant win prizes (explained later in the chapter). The contest ran for 90 days and also awarded manager level prizes for the stores that performed the best.

The contest results were staggering - a 15-30% increase in the items sold which resulted in over $900,000 in incremental sales (about 1.5%) for the quarter. The total cost of the contest was $90,000 ($18,000 fixed cost for lottery-style tickets and communication and $72,000 for prizes). After the contest, the sales of those items slipped anywhere from 10% – 25% from the contest averages, but still in excess of pre-contest results by 10% – 15%.

The benefits of the contest were realized long after the cost of the contest ended. Those payouts keep giving you a return on your investment even after the expenses of the contests have ended.

Ever heard the investment term *"arbitrage?"*
It simply means, *"a return without risk."*

In this case, the fixed costs were $18,000 – the total money at risk ($60 per restaurant). By setting the reward hurdle at the historical levels, you do not spend anything extra if you receive nothing incremental. There is little risk (in this example $60 per store) to setting up the program this way. The performers shine and get rewards. Soon, the Blinking Stars catch on and start driving the business and earning prizes. The Anchors continue to complain (but we spend nothing on them!). Follow these simple guidelines to earn your business some incredible financial returns with virtually no downside!

Years of refining and running contests have led to these critical items if you're getting ready to implement a contest.

INCENTIVE CONTEST
KEYS FOR SUCCESS

1 **Do not use cash as the only prize!** – As mentioned earlier, if cash/salary/bonuses worked, every tipped or commissioned employee would be a top salesperson. Cash covers the employees' basic needs, but is not a primary motivator to excel in their performance.

2 **Set a "hurdle" or "base" rate to exceed your current levels (i.e. lowering cost or driving sales)** – The key to making arbitrage work. Reward only those who exceed it (for selling) or lower it (for costs). To get the contest to pay out financially, you do not want to pay for performance you are already receiving. This strategy limits (nearly zeroes out) your downside – you only pay out when they beat the goal. You can generate a guaranteed financial return. Do not reward average performance. Most systems (or a spreadsheet program) can provide basic information that helps track what employees are selling.

Reward BOTH the Managers and Employees – At minimum, reward the employees – they are the ones making it happen. *Do not* reward just the managers – bad message to the employees. Remember, typically your employees mimic your managers – ensure there is something in it for them – everyone heading in the same direction. Everyone wants to win the big prize no matter what level in the company. That is why frequent flier/buyer programs are so successful – people go out of their way (i.e. above and beyond) to get those points!

Track it – People like to know how they are doing. All sports teams keep score to monitor progress. A little progress (in the right direction) each day is still progress. Send out frequent updates. People may think they are doing well until they see how others are faring. We all anxiously await our next frequent flier/shopper statements to see if we have moved up to the next level.

Provide "more of less" – Rewarding many people with even a small award (time pass, free food, etc.) will drive results much faster than setting a big grand prize only one person can win. While "one-of-a-kind" trips and prizes sound exciting and may garner an initial reaction, it wears off quickly as employees realize it is extremely hard (or lucky) to win. The incremental rewards along the way will promote competition between divisions or within oneself to keep reaching for the next level. With one large random reward, there is no direct tie from performance to reward. While there is a place for large awards as the 'ultimate carrot', do not forget to reward *all* the employees who improved their performance (and your sales and profits). If you have limited resources, take some of the cost out of the grand prize and spread it amongst smaller prizes more people can win. Or, better yet, have a vendor partner share in the cost. How did you feel the last time you bought a lottery ticket?

Set 3-4 different reward levels and ratchet up the payouts – For example, if an employee sells $200 (above current trends) in additional items, they get a $10 gift certificate (five cents on the dollar), but if they sell $500, they get a $30 gift certificate (six cents on the dollar). The more they sell, the more they win (and so do you). For those with employees that deal with larger sales, the process works the same, only with larger numbers. The same approach can be taken in lowering costs as a business objective (i.e. reward 10 cents for every dollar saved).

7 Have the employees wear buttons/pins – "If I don't suggest _____, you get a free _____!" (or a similar style of button/pin relating to guest service, etc.). In retail stores, these could be used to build behaviors to ask for "Instant Credit" (signing up for that store's credit card) or for Extended Warranty programs. Restaurant employees can wear them to promote a specific food or drink item. Any service industry could wear these for "Catch me doing something right" type programs. The button (and your guests/clients) will manage the employee in a fun way when you are not around.

The definition of integrity is...
"What you do when nobody is watching."

This button/pin ensures someone is always watching. Try this suggestion and watch your guests'/clients' faces – they are just hoping your employee makes a mistake. I frequent a Diamond Shamrock convenience store in my neighborhood and they have their cashiers wearing a $1 bill on their uniform, as well as a button that says if they fail to suggest a drink when you buy chips (or vice versa), you get the dollar. *Every time* I buy a soda there, they always ask if I need some chips or a lottery ticket to go with the soda. Their sales of those items have dramatically increased. Everyone could use those results.

The U.S. Post Office in my neighborhood has even gotten in on the action. Every time someone mails a package, the person working the desk always asks if you would like delivery confirmation or insurance (additional sales for the Postmaster). Their employees have to understand why they need to do this, as well as how it impacts the company (and their employment). Should they pay a little extra for those that sell? Yes! It's silly to think that all employees will follow these steps every transaction without a little extra incentive. The company is collecting additional revenue each time the employee asks and converts the sale. The employees need to suggest critical sales items. Since you (the manager) cannot be a part of every transaction, these buttons can help in a fun way.

8 Begin a point program and use 'Company Bucks' or 'pull-tab' tickets – The employees can either earn points/bucks toward specific items, a chance for cash or collect and save the pull-tab tickets for bigger prizes. While many companies have some sort of program, often times the bucks or points are given out very subjectively. Link quantifiable business goals such as sales or profit increases to the reward of these cards or points. Pull-tab cards are lottery-style cards that you remove three to four tabs to reveal a line of shapes similar to a slot machine. If you match three-of-a-kind, that ticket is worth a certain amount of points. If you use the pull-tab cards, make the "loser" cards worth something (i.e. 1 point). The pull-tab cards can be purchased in

lots of 1000 for about 1.5 cents each and they contain random shapes. Match three-of-a-kind to win. The quantity of matches of the different shapes are outlined in the box, so you can set the point values of each different three-of-a-kind and set up the prize levels accordingly to ensure a proper return.

You often see consumer promotions along these lines: come into the store on a specific date, bring the items you would like to purchase to the register and have the sales clerk scratch off the hidden discount on your card. You cannot lose! The store had to spend some money (the discount) to get you in the door. Better in their door than the competition's door! You can use the same approach with the pull-tab (or scratch-off type cards) – they are worth various values based on what is revealed and the employees save them for larger prizes.

9 **Ensure the prizes are what Employees (not you) want** – Find out what the people participating in the program would like as prizes. Too often, someone sitting in an office that is from a different generation selects the prizes for the program. Your employees may not want a crystal vase or grandfather clock with your company logo on it as a grand prize. Survey employees and find out what types of awards they would like at different prize levels.

10 **Conduct an auction with the points** – A neat twist on the point/buck program is to sporadically put cool prize items up for bid. Your employees can bid against each other for the items similar to an online auction. Not only will your employees earn some cool prizes, they will have a great time bidding to win. In addition, the bidding in most cases will cause the employees to spend more points relative to the value of the item, so you will save a few dollars.

Partner with vendors, suppliers and distributors – Let them pay for a portion of the contest or provide logoed items. You are selling more of their product, let them help pay for those additional sales! Often times, they will provide a rebate for the amount sold over the prior year. You can utilize this money to pay for big-ticket prizes. Alternatively, they can provide their own logoed items as prizes.

Use gift certificates/cards for prizes – Restaurants, gas cards, movie passes, clothing, music & video stores. Many of these establishments will offer a discount – an incredible value to stretch your contest dollar! As mentioned earlier there are a number of vendors that offer many choices all on one gift certificate – the employee can choose which gift they want.

Do not make the "losers" pay for the winners' prizes – Some companies try to net out the cost of the prizes by having the losers pay for the cost of the winners' prizes – the worse you do, the more you pay. Not very motivating for them. Their performance might not be the best, but it improved – and that is what you want!

Follow through – Ensure the contest is running smoothly and results are being communicated quickly. Finally, make the presentation of the prizes an event and ensure all recipients actually receive their awards in a timely fashion. The way the award is given can make or break the employees' trust factor. Nothing is worse than an insincere gift.

NOTE: Let me stress the importance of the Point Programs, 'Company Bucks' or Pull-Tab tickets. While your initial reaction may be to balk at the expense of obtaining the cards or 'bucks', they give your managers incredible flexibility to adapt the program to their specific needs, as well as the ability to reward all employees in their department or store, not just the ones participating in a sales contest.

WHO GETS THE FLOWERS?

When designing an incentive contest, the worst thing you could do is simply reward the manager. It will further solidify your employees' beliefs that all the glory, money and recognition is given to the one on top. Conversely, if you only reward the employees, you will not be answering the "What's in it for me?" question that may be asked by the managers. The manager is driving the team, as well as being the point person for communication to the team, It is critical to reward all levels. You need the employees who do the work being reinforced by the managers who follow-up and are focused on the same objectives.

The spirit of competition (to beat other parts of the company or one's own personal records) will drive the success of the program. No matter what level anyone is within the organization, they all want to be recognized and appreciated for making a difference in achieving the business goals of the company. This strategy will go a long way in quieting any issues you have between the top levels getting all the perks, while the bottom levels do all the work. With that in mind, let us look at a contest you could run in your company to put your money where your mouth is and jumpstart the recognition culture movement.

EASY TO IMPLEMENT CONTEST

While Appendix A focuses on specific types of contests that can be designed and implemented, potential uses for them and the pros and cons of each type of contest, this chapter outlines an easy to implement "Save and Win" program in which you can simply track results on a spreadsheet, or use pull-tab cards or 'Company Bucks.' All of the contests have been tried and tested so find the best type for your business environment.

SIMPLE SAVE AND WIN PROGRAM

As discussed earlier, you will need to set hurdle rates if you are going to implement a sales-driving or cost-containment program. There is no need to reward the performance you are already getting from the team. On the profit side, reward performance that generates costs savings above the current rate. In its simplest format (and one easy to implement within a single unit or department), you may set some objectives for the contest that could include:

- **Suggestive selling of a specific item or items** – Sales Teams: new items, monthly features, high-margin items. Retail: Instant Credits or extended warranties. Restaurants: Desserts, premium brands of alcohol, appetizers, value meal upsells, etc. Vendors: Reward distributors for product sales over historical levels. Not only will they increase sales of your items, it will decrease sales of your competitors! Do not forget to set hurdle rates that will motivate employees to strive to exceed today's current performance and ensure you receive the necessary return on investment.

- **Cost/Waste or other Profit Targets** - to reward those that may not have a direct impact on top line, but certainly on the bottom line. Most employees impact profitability at some level – whether through proper cost containment or their own productivity. Design programs that reward the team or individual for beating current cost parameters (without sacrificing quality) within their direct control.

- **Company-wide cost reductions** - During tough financial times, set up a cost reduction program to reward employees who provide suggestions that are implemented. This approach is perceived far more positively than the typical budget cutbacks and spending/wage freezes normally seen. Isn't it ironic to see a company cut pennies down at the lower levels to the point where their people do not even have the tools to do their jobs, yet the top brass does not play by the same rules. What kind of message does that send? People are smart enough to understand the explanation that times are tight and everyone needs to conserve a little. This system, though, rewards positive behaviors even in down times.

Remember, $1 in sales does not equal $1 in profit, but $1 in reduced expenses is $1 in profit.

- **Safety** – Avoiding costly accidents saves the company plenty in claims and lost hours. It is simple to see if this pays out. Reward the employees for safe days and see how much money you save in workers' compensation claims, legal fees/lawsuits and lost productivity and work time.

- **Driving sales of new products**

- **Attendance / Timeliness**

- **Uniform Compliance** – what has "casual Friday" eroded to in your office?

- **Mystery Shopper scores**

- **Utilizing guests' names at key moments** (i.e. thanking guest who paid with a credit card) if it is a service standard within your company.

- **Cook/Delivery/Production times** (i.e. get 100 points per employee if production times do not go over ___ minutes, or their deliveries are made within a specified time). After all, time is money. As good as you may be, there is still room for improvement.

- **Training skills of employees** – "Pass the test and/or demonstrate the skill" and receive ___ points. Can also be used as an incentive to learn other skills (i.e. software, etc.) that will benefit the business.

- **Breakage or Over/Short** – Minimize breakage/waste under ____%, or stay within ___ cents and receive ____ points. The average bank teller loses over $250 per year! For those of you who deal with warehouse employees, production/assembly line workers, shipping departments or cash handlers, reward them for being close to the mark.

- **Cleanliness** – "Find the Dot, Clean the Spot™" is a unique program to drive cleanliness in your warehouse, restaurant, office or distribution facility. Have the manager place little round stickers in various hard to see and/or dirty places. Every employee who "finds a dot and cleans the spot" will receive a specified point value. You will be amazed to see the difference in attitudes towards 'menial' tasks such as these when managers reward the efforts of their team. Similar approaches can be taken in other areas such as finding product defects, errors in manuals and safety violations.

- **Positive comments on guest comment cards/surveys/e-mail**

- **Finishing projects prior to a deadline or rewarding hourly employees for finishing their closing duties early (or any opportunity you have for hourly employees to get done early).** A little extra incentive to get done early saves you money and allows people to move on to the next project.

It can definitely be argued all of the above are part of every employee's job description (selling, being profit-conscious, coming to work in proper attire, being on time, practicing safe work habits, cleaning as you go, etc.) and they should be doing what we pay them to do. By focusing on a few of these key items in your place of business, it will show how serious you are about these items. By rewarding employees, you will show the Shining Stars and Blinking Stars that you value their contributions over the average and below-average performer.

The following example uses a fast food restaurant scenario for ease of analysis – we have all eaten at one and understand the terminology and mathematics of the contest. The same template can be used to drive sales of any product in any environment when you have someone who interfaces with a guest/client regarding purchases or upgrades of your products and/or services (phone or in person). These types of programs are ideal to supplement product launches and/or marketing initiatives or can be modified for use in a cost-reduction program. The two-pronged approach of the marketing push along with the additional rewards geared towards the sales force will ensure higher sales and greater returns for the company.

RESTAURANT SALES CONTEST

Joey's Fast Food sells value meals and offers the option to "Big Joey-size" them. The Joey-size moves you from a medium fries and drink to a large  fries and drink. Currently, they charge 49 cents for the upgrade and make an incremental profit of 25 cents. They currently sell 3,000 value meals per week and 300 of them get "Joey-sized" (10% are upgraded). All his cashiers swear they ask every guest if they want to "Joey-size" their order. Big Joey is a little skeptical.

Big Joey wants to raise that percentage to 30%. He's tried retraining, yelling, screaming and demanding to no avail. Additionally, his cashier over-short is an alarming $50 per week. Money is coming in the front door, but going out the back door.

Joey reads this book and sets up the following contest:

Cashiers who sell more than 1 "Joey-size" meal for every 10 value meals sold (current 10% sell rate) receive 1 point, as long as their over / short is less than $.50 that day. If they are missing too much money, they do not receive the points for that day. The cashiers can save points to receive the following items:

    200 Points = $5 Video Store Gift Card

    500 Points = $15 Movie Gift Certificate or Restaurant Gift Card

    1000 Points = $35 Dinner for Two or Gas Card

FINANCIAL ANALYSIS

For a cashier to earn 200 points, they must sell 200 more "Joey-size" meals than they currently do today. That generates an additional $98 in sales

(200 x \$.49 ea.) and \$50 in profit (200 x \$.25 ea.) for Big Joey. He then pays out a \$5 video store gift card. The cashiers are basically earning 5 cents on the incremental sales dollar (or 10 cents of incremental profit) generated on these items – a pretty good commission as a fast food cashier. If their over-short is too high, they lose the points. My guess is that his over-short problem will go away as well. More good news – those who do not sell above the current average receive nothing (unfortunately, so does Joey – in the form of lost sales).

The example used here is for simplicity's sake. You can take the same principles and template and use them for your business:

- Obtain historical results

- Set desired payouts/incentives for exceeding past individual or team performance

- Implement the plan with the team

- Track and communicate the results often

- Conduct analysis at the end of the program and get feedback from the team to see what worked and what didn't

- Tweak it for the next time.

For more examples of specific types of contests, see Appendix A.

WHAT YOU WILL SEE

If you design the contest correctly, you should see the following things occur:

1) **Results (sales and profit) increase** – whatever you are focusing on during the contest period (i.e. suggesting "Joey-size" meals).

2) **Results will taper off after the contest is over** – but not to the levels prior to the contest.

3) **Employee enthusiasm and ownership** – Generates a great 'vibe' towards the company and its guests/clients/customers and is something other employers don't do. They are now receiving a 'fraction of the action.'

4) **Turnover decrease** – If the contest is cool enough (and prizes are redeemed only at the end), people will stick around until the contest is over. It is up to you to ensure they continue to stay.

5) **Your stars will perform as they have in the past, at even higher levels** – The Blinking-Stars will move it up a notch. The Anchors will complain the contest is stupid and quit (hopefully). Time to 'average up' when you hire their replacements.

6) **Morale should improve** - the team is performing and being rewarded for it.

When you implement contests, ensure the timeframe is not too long. Employees will lose interest if the chance to earn rewards is further out than 30 days. If you do want to put together a program for a full quarter, ensure there are opportunities during the program for the employees to redeem their points and receive the recognition prior to the end of the quarter.

Now it is time to look at the "Full Bouquet" – designing a recognition system that is easy to implement and track to ensure you provide the company culture to your team that they deserve. For specific help regarding how you could utilize the ideas presented here, drop a line to **tj@thepeoplepyramid.com.**

THE FULL BOUQUET

You have seen how contests can impact your business, now let's look at putting together a comprehensive employee loyalty program. Many companies have some sort of formalized recognition program for service awards. The challenge is to create a complete loyalty and recognition system for your company to keep dangling the carrot (one they can catch with great performance) and keep your people rewarded and happy – working for you, not the competition.

The following type of system can be tailored to people in sales, offices, warehouses, delivery drivers, restaurants, retail stores or hotels – hourly or salary, production worker or manager/supervisor. It rewards employees for even the most basic of functions, but ensures those that do perform get rewarded (and stay). Send your employees "the full bouquet!"

BIG JOEY'S PROGRAM

Now that Big Joey has completed some successful sales campaigns, he is ready for the final step. He has set up a complete program focusing on his business objectives, as well as the service awards program.

Though Joey runs a restaurant, this same template can be used with slight modifications to be effective in virtually any business environment. You know what is important to track in your business. Big Joey has chosen to reward the following items:

1) **Attendance** – Points for no missed days, as well as being on time.

2) **Uniform compliance** – Points for showing up in complete attire.

3) **Tenure** – Receive points for each 3 months of tenure.

4) **Suggestive Selling (for cashiers)** – Points for selling specific items over historic rates.

5) **Food Cost / Waste (for kitchen crew)** – Points for achieving weekly food cost goals and minimal waste.

POINT SYSTEM (or Company Bucks)

The crew of Big Joey's restaurant can earn the following points in each area:

1) **ATTENDANCE** – Showing up for all scheduled shifts for the month earns you 100 points. Additionally, they earn an additional 5 points (per shift) for not being more than 5 minutes late for the shift.

2) **UNIFORM COMPLIANCE** – Earn 5 points for each shift they show up in complete uniform.

3) **TENURE** – Receive 100 points for every 3 months of tenure.

4) **SUGGESTIVE SELLING** – Receive 1 point for each Big Joey size meal sold over the new 25% hurdle rate.

5) **FOOD COST** – Earn 100 points if the team makes less than 10 mistakes per week and an additional 200 points if food cost is +/- 0.1% the target percentage or 100 points if between +/-0.11% and 0.3%

6) **EMPLOYEE OF THE DAY** – Manager on duty rewards 25 points for the employee of the day.

EXAMPLE

Susie works 12 shifts during the month of June (and did not miss one). She is on time for every shift AND in complete uniform (It can happen!). She hits her 90-day anniversary during the month and sold 200 Big Joey size meals over her hurdle rate of 25%. She earns:

ATTENDANCE –	12 shifts x 5 pts. each =	60 pts.
ATTENDANCE –	Didn't miss a shift =	100 pts.
UNIFORMS –	12 shifts x 5 pts. per =	60 pts.
SUGG. SELLING – 200 x 1 pt.	=	200 pts.
	TOTAL	420 pts.
ANNIVERSARY –	3 months	= 100 pts.

Showing up for every shift, being on time, in uniform and suggestive selling earns her 520 points for the month. While it may have initially seemed odd to you to reward an employee for something so basic, by now you should realize the impact this can have on your company.

Big Joey has devised the following prize values for his crew:

LEVEL	CHOICE OF ONE
600 points	$10 Video Gift Card 60-minute phone card Big Joey T-Shirt 120-minute get out of work free card
1500 points	$25 Gas Card Movie Pass for Two (w/popcorn and sodas) $25 Web Super-Certificate
2500 points	$50 Gas Card $50 Web Super-Certificate Walkman-style Player Paid Day Off
5000 points	$100 Web Super-Certificate Leather Big Joey Bomber Jacket 13" TV/VCR Combo

If Susie continues her impressive performance each month, she would earn 5440 points over the course of 12 months (at 420 points per month plus the 100 points for each 3 months of tenure). It would cost Big Joey roughly $100 in prizes she will have redeemed. While $100 might seem expensive to pay someone for doing their job, it is much cheaper than recruiting, hiring and training a new employee. Additionally, Big Joey will be receiving additional sales and profit from her awesome suggestive selling (additional 200 meals per month on her shifts), as well as the stability in guest service by having the same employee serving guests month in and month out. The profit payout alone on the additional meals sold is 200 per month times $0.25 profit per meal. Annualized over twelve months will net a total increase in profit due to Susie's selling of $600!

As you can see, Big Joey is a firm believer in the programs discussed here. Not only is he realizing the additional benefits of incremental sales and profits, he is also going to see reduced costs due to lower turnover/enhanced tenure and, finally, increased guest satisfaction. This example assumes no increase in guest frequency generated from this enhanced level of service and stability.

While the example used here is simplistic, all of us eat in restaurants and can understand the concepts used here. If your team deals directly with product sales (no matter what they are), you can use a simple contest like the one in Chapter 8. The 'full bouquet' program described here can be tailored to any business environment. Pick the top 4-5 business goals/objectives and design the system to reward employees for their performance.

WHAT ABOUT THE MANAGERS?

It is strongly recommended that Big Joey (and yourself) setup a program for the managers of the store/department/warehouse, especially if they are not on a bonus program (i.e. Assistant Managers and hourly or line-level supervisors). Add the following to your program:

1) **Divide your employees into 2-3 teams (or as many managers as you have).**

2) **Reward the managers based on their TEAM'S performance (i.e. they receive points if ALL their employees show up for their shifts, are in uniform, on time, beat sales goals).**

3) **Make minor modifications to tailor the program to your Company. For example, replace the TENURE section with a TURNOVER section. If their team loses 1 person or less, they receive 200 points, 2-3 people, they get 100 points and over 3 they get 0.**

4) **The manager with the most "Employees of the Day" or top salesperson could earn additional points.**

Are these different ways to approach running a group of employees? Certainly! Does it work? You bet! Will it solve all your problems? Not entirely, but it will help you make enormous strides towards achieving your goals. Does it cost you money? Sure it does. Get over the "cost" of the prize and focus on all the benefits the program gives you, your employees, your guests and your wallet.

HOW DOES THIS WORK FOR YOU?

Here are a few examples of how you can reward performance in various business scenarios:

SALES TEAMS

- Exceeding sales quotas for the week/month/quarter
- Lower overhead or departmental budget expenses
- Driving sales of new or higher margin products
- Reward distributors or clients as well as your own salespeople
- Promotions or new job title

WAREHOUSES

- Safety programs
- Cost/inventory containment
- Decrease in breakage or pilferage
- Loading/unloading in record times
- Cleanliness
- Attendance/uniform compliance
- Promotions or new job title

OFFICES

- Attendance, dress code
- Department goals
- Productivity (i.e. for payroll, data entry or A/P clerks)
- Cost containment ideas – office supplies, overhead reduction, utilities, etc.

RESTAURANTS / RETAIL

- "VIG" (Very Important Guest) Cards – Have employees pass these fliers/cards out to friends, neighbors, etc. The employee signs their name on each one and then they receive points/prizes for them when redeemed. Everyone is a salesperson!

- Attendance – Showing up for all shifts

- Attendance – Timeliness

- Uniform Compliance

- Safety – Days without injuries/accidents

- Tenure

- Training – Completion of initial program / passing tests

- Product Cost / Waste Tracking

- "TEAM" closes – getting done by a specific time earns points

- Validations – Re-validating various skill levels

- Mystery Shopper/Guest Comment Letters and Cards

- Promotion to Trainer or Supervisor

FULL SERVICE RESTAURANT APPLICATIONS

- Upselling various items – Large drinks, appetizers, desserts, premium liquor.

- Cook Times (If orders do not go over a specified time, kitchen team earns points); product quality or plate presentations.

- Hostesses – Focus on suggesting specials, appetizers, soups or desserts. If the team exceeds the base amount for the day (they plant the seed for the guest), they get rewarded.

QUICK SERVICE RESTAURANT APPLICATIONS

- Upsell value meals, extra cheese on pizza or desserts – most quick serve restaurants upgrade less than 15% of their value meal orders. Plenty of lost sales dollars there!

- Cook times under a specific time; product quality; no waste
- Drive Thru or Delivery times under a specific time
- Cashier over/short

HOTEL APPLICATIONS

- Food and beverage units can setup similar systems to those previously discussed
- Housekeeping – reward for showing up, observations/follow-up scores, guest comments, productivity above current levels, cost reduction suggestions
- Front Desk – reward for using guest's names (or other business objectives), attendance, check out times
- Valets/Bellman – reward attendance, guest feedback/comments, productivity

Setting up a program for your Company takes a little time on the front end, but will pay off many times over. If you're not sure about it, start small – maybe a sales contest or a cost-containment program for your team. Eventually, you will be setting up the "Full Bouquet" of flowers for your employees. These programs and contests are critical to jumpstart the culture shift within your organization. Employees have seen managers try to change so many things over the years - they're suspicious. Put your money where your mouth is to back up how important this cultural shift is to you and the company.

CONCLUSION

Creating a recognition culture takes time and commitment from all levels of an organization. Contests are an simple way to lay the foundation for your employees to begin feeling safe in this new culture and strengthen their trust in you. Studies have shown it takes 21 days to change a behavior. You will have to practice giving praise for three weeks until it becomes a habit. To change the momentum that is your current culture within your organization takes repeated efforts over time. Recognize now, recognize often!

Those Blinking Stars will need that same length of time to get used to the new system and to be recognized for their performance (which, initially, will not be each and everyday). You can make a difference within your company or department. If you are on the bottom of the ladder or in the middle of the organization, remember the earlier tip about training your boss by prompting praise from them.

Adopt a similar approach that marketers have used for years by focusing on the heavy users. You too can be successful with your people. All you have to do is spend time with the performers instead of your non-performers. Setup a 'frequent flier' system for your employees. Praise and recognize them and watch the results. Let them earn points or win contests – you will be driving the sales and profit within the organization while allowing your people to be appreciated for their contributions – all three parts of the wheel will be moving the same direction. Who knows, maybe your employees will think you are from the same planet they are! For some, it is a dramatic shift in management styles. Stay the course and reap the benefits.

As mentioned earlier in the book, your behavior must match your beliefs. Do not fool yourself into thinking contests and rewards will create the culture by themselves. You cannot fake or buy character and sincerity. If you do not mean it, do not do it. You need to show your employees you care. The behavior (your actions) must match your belief in this way of managing. If not, your employees will see right through it. If you think a contest will turn the tide, it can – but only with the cooperation of management starting the process of recognizing performance. Believe in this method and behave in the same manner – you, your company and your employees will benefit.

SWING THE PENDULUM

A friend of mine, Roger Cardinale talks about behaviors as a pendulum. Changing the culture or environment in an organization or single business location is like trying to change the direction of a pendulum. If the pendulum is moving in a certain direction or is far from the center, you have to push extra hard (over-exaggerate the movement) to get it to swing back the other direction. The same can be said for trying to change the current culture within an organization. If the environment lacks the things mentioned here, you will have to work extra hard to move them (swing the pendulum) the other way.

Ideas such as contests and incentive programs can actually be the catalyst to swing the pendulum back the other way – they will help you 'over-exaggerate' the movements needed to get your team to start believing in this new philosophy. Explaining it to your team in this manner is simple for them to understand so they can get on the same side as you in pushing the momentum back the right way. Avoid the pitfalls mentioned throughout the book and leverage your time and efforts on the items that are effective.

Since you are over-exaggerating the movements to begin with, be careful it does not swing too far the other way. An analogy of this situation would be an introductory price to get consumers to purchase your product. The initial offer starts a frenzy of buying (swinging the pendulum), but if you do not slow it down or stop it, the consumers may only buy at this low price. At that point, you are not making any money, as the pendulum has swung too far the other way.

Contests and extra incentive programs are great to get things started, but once the culture is beginning to take hold, make the goals more challenging and raise the bar to ensure people do not tire of the system. We want to keep the pendulum in the center, as well as the sales, people, profit wheel in total balance. Minor modifications along the way are necessary to keep the programs and the returns coming. After all, a bouquet of flowers only lasts so long! Change the 'flowers' around, hold a points auction, shift the focus occasionally – people get tired of the same thing day in and day out.

This book is a compilation of my years of work in the service and incentive industry. Will you agree with all of the ideas or be able to apply them all? No. Take the best ones that will work in your specific situation and begin there. Soon, you will be an even more successful manager and drive great sales, service and profits for your company.

Since most of us were never managed in this way, it is tough to break the cycle. Stop complaining and start training (your boss, that is). Ask those leading questions we discussed early and impact the people within your direct control. You will earn a stellar reputation for achieving incredible results - the right way. Soon, people will want to work for you and you will have a larger number of people to manage and teach this new philosophy.

The beauty of this system is in its balance. Often times, companies are too results-driven or too people-driven. By implementing this strategy, you will ensure all the business goals and objectives are met (addressing the need for sales and profit results), while keeping all your good people happy (addressing the people needs). The list of companies that excel in this area is short. Begin today so you too can join that list.

To be successful with this strategy, start small – within your span of control. Next, train your boss with leading questions based on your team's enhanced performance levels. Everyone will be talking about the success you are having. If you impact 10 people in 3 months of practicing this strategy and those people each impact 10 more in the next 3 months and so on, in 18 months, you will have impacted over 1 million people! Start the pendulum swinging and the momentum rolling with just 10 people. It can happen!

As with any book you read or seminar you attend, the adrenaline rush of new ideas often gets quickly managed out of you upon your return to the daily grind. Commit to not letting that fire get blown out – do something and do it quickly! Get the pendulum swinging and create that 'frequent-flier' mentality within your group immediately. Do not waiver, accept nothing less than the results you desire!

The opportunity to move up and affect more people will grow the new culture over time and help your company become even more successful. Don't wait until it is too late to "Send Flowers to the Living"!

OTHER TYPES OF CONTESTS

As in the earlier examples, we are again using a fast food restaurant for simplicity sake. The sales scenario is easy to comprehend, as are the financial implications. In addition, this example flows from the earlier one. You can then modify this template to fit your business. Whether you choose to use pull-tab cards, 'Company Bucks' or simply track points on a spreadsheet, these types of programs are very effective. You will however, need to change small portions of it to keep it fresh.

COLLECT AND WIN CONTESTS

Big Joey has just had a rousing success with his suggestive selling contest. The contest is over and his numbers are beginning to subside from the 40% sell rate during the contest. They are currently running at 25% (far in excess of the 10% prior to the contest) – his cashiers want another contest! Additionally, his other employees want to participate in these incentive programs as well.

Looking back through the book, he decides to implement another type of contest and purchases a few boxes of 1000 pull-tab tickets (you can use 'Company Buck' or simply track points on a spreadsheet just as easy. However, you lose the lottery feel of winning big) and sets up the following contest objectives:

1) **CASHIERS – Reward "Joey-size" meals that exceed 25% (new current rate)**

2) **KITCHEN – Start each shift with potential to earn 50 tickets. Lose 1 ticket each time a drive-thru time goes over 1 minute (his current target), as well as losing a ticket for each incorrect order.**

As you can see, he has now raised the bar for the cashiers. They now receive the reward only if they sell over 25% (their current level of performance). In the previous contest, they were rewarded above the 10% level. The box of 1000 tickets has 5 different shapes that have the following number of three-of-a-kind:

MATCH	# IN BOX	
3 Diamonds	2	(Out of 1000 cards in the box)
3 Hearts	5	
3 Triangles	25	
3 Squares	100	
3 Circles	250	
No 3 of-a-kind	618	
TOTAL	**1000**	

Joey, keen math whiz that he is, sets up the following point scale for the cards:

MATCH	VALUE	#IN BOX	TOTAL PTS.
3 Diamonds	250 pts.	2	500
3 Hearts	150 pts.	5	750
3 Triangles	100 pts.	25	2500
3 Squares	25 pts.	100	2500
3 Circles	10 pts.	250	2500
No 3 of-a-kind	1 pt.	618	618
	TOTAL	**1000 Cards**	**9368 Pts.**

Following his logic, if someone won all 1000 cards, they would receive 9368 points. Therefore, if someone receives one card, on average, they would win 9.368 points.

Knowing that, he set up the following prizes:

1800 pts. = $5 Video Store Gift Card or Free Meals for 5 Shifts

3000 pts. = $10 Movie Certificate or $10 Phone Card

8000 pts. = $30 Electronic Store Gift Certificate or a Paid Day Off

The contest begins and is much harder for the cashiers, but the performers still win many cards. Since they do not receive cards unless they clear the hurdle rate of 25% upgrades, Big Joey gives out no prizes (translation, spends no money) unless they exceed that rate. The kitchen crew is incredibly excited and turns in record cook times (hopefully translating into return guest visits – albeit hard to quantify), and helps minimize waste to earn prizes (easy to quantify). More money on the top flows more money to the bottom.

FINANCIAL ANALYSIS

A cashier who was selling 25% upsells, now moves to 35% due to the new incentive. She now sells 100 more for every 1000 meals she rings up. That translates into $49 in sales and $25 in profit for Big Joey. She would receive 100 tickets for that performance. On average, she would receive approximately 937 points. If she sells 200 over her current level, she would earn approximately 1800 points – enough for the $5 gift card (exact same payout as the last contest). There would be an additional cost for the cards of about $15 per box of 1000. Remember, he is still far in excess of the 10% rate he was originally selling. His old contest is really still paying out for him.

PROS

This type of contest will have the following benefits:

- Can use the cards (or 'Company bucks') for many things in other areas of the business as mentioned earlier – cleanliness, kitchen cook times, having people come in early or stay late (on the clock of course), uniform compliance, etc. You can use these to reward the business goals setup to be rewarded, as well as having them available to all senior execs to use at their discretion.

- Adds the excitement of the lottery – "I could get the big winner."

- You could make the three-of-a-kind with the least number of cards in the box worth some huge number. Simply rework the prize levels accordingly based on the average points of the tickets in the box.

- You can set the point values for each match at whatever you desire. Make sure you do the math so the contest pays itself off. If it is too easy, the company will not generate adequate returns. If it is too difficult, employees will lose interest and it will fail.

- Make sure the "loser" cards (those with no three-of-a-kind) are worth at least one point. After all, people performing at a level high enough to earn these cards are well in excess of current performance rates – they need a reward.

CONS

- Additional cost of the cards (about 1.5 cents each), but it is worth it. Alternatively, you could print your own 'Company bucks'. They lose a little of the randomness and 'big-win' potential, but are less expensive.

- Set up a simple spreadsheet updated weekly with the point totals so the employees do not have to save all their tickets.

- Managers start using them to "bribe" employees to do things – is that a bad thing?

- Some analysis is required to determine point values and prize levels to ensure financial returns are met.

These contests do require a little work and some math on the front-end to ensure the point values and the prize levels work out. The payoff of these contests is seeing the employees pulling the tabs off each card to see if they won. Remember, ensure the "loser" cards (no 3 of-a-kind) are worth at least 1 point, otherwise, you will have fewer winners – just like the lottery!

NOTE: Although there is an additional cost due to the cards/bucks, it is recommended they be utilized in any program you setup. The biggest plus is the ability to use them for any specific needs your business has outside the main program. For example, you could use them to reward the salesperson's assistant as they definitely impact that person's ability to sell more product. Try it with the cards/bucks and then without – wait to see the disappointment on the employees' faces if they can't save and win.

In regards to prizes, you can setup a system as simple as this one (and manage it in-house to save expenses) or you could hire an incentive company to manage the system for you. They would be happy to provide a catalog full of prizes, as well as produce the materials to distribute to your employees. The benefit of using a catalog-type approach is you don't have to manage, nor are responsible for the inventory. The downside is the additional cost to have someone helping you. If you are short on time, go this route. If you are short on money, manage it as simply as possible to ensure as much of that money goes into the rewards versus the administering of the program.

GAME BOARD (or Bingo card)

Restaurants and supermarkets have used this as a marketing strategy for quite a long time to build guest frequency. Buy their value meals (or other specified items) and receive some tickets that can be opened to reveal different game pieces. You simply have to collect the specified pieces (i.e. collect piece 44 and 45 to win $5,000) to win. As we all know, there are 1,000,000 of piece 44 printed and only 1 of piece 45 – ensuring one winner (maybe), and a whole bunch of hopefuls. You can try this fun spin on your contests in the following two ways:

A) SMALLER COMPANY

Create your own game board or bingo card and have the different "properties" be various menu items that can be sold. You can set various quantities (values) for each property. For example, sell 100 Joey-size meals and you earn square 1. Sell 100 more and earn square 2. Once you've collected those two squares, you win a $5 gift certificate.

JOEY LANE Upsell 100 Joey-Size Meals	JOEY AVENUE Upsell 100 More Joey-Size Meals	MRS. JOEY ROAD Sell 25 Milk Shakes	MRS. JOEY COURT Sell 25 Apple Pies
JOEY-LAND Collect Joey Ln. + Joey Ave. = $5 Gift Certificate Collect Mrs. Joey Rd. + Mrs. Joey Ct. = $10 Gift Certificate Collect Vinnie Pl. + Vinnie St. = $20 Gift Certificate Collect Mama Ln. + Mama Rd. = $30 Gift Certificate			
VINNIE PLACE Sell 50 Orders of the New Buffalo Wings	VINNIE STREET Sell 50 Large Salads VS. Small Salads	MAMA LANE Sell 25 Gift Certificates ($5 Each)	MAMA ROAD Sell 50 Double Meat Burgers

You can obviously set up the squares to be whatever products or goals you want. Set the quotas so you are selling more of the items than you are today. Put the higher profit and/or harder to sell items at the end of your game, so to win the big prize, they'll really have to make you some money.

Alternatively, you could create a bingo card and the employees cover the squares as they successfully complete them. You can customize the squares into any business or personal goal – driving sales, containing costs, learning new skills or software, attendance, personal records, etc.

B) LARGER CHAIN

If you can afford to print your own game board and pieces (about 1.5 cents each for a quantity of 500,000 total), you could create an incredibly cool game for your employees. Simply set your goals and hurdle rates and then hand out game pieces when those rates are exceeded (i.e. one piece for each item sold over the hurdle rate). The employees would try to then collect each piece to win (i.e. Collect piece 1,2,3 to win a jacket; Collect 4,5,6 to win a golf shirt).

The advantage to the board game is you have a set number of winners, so you know your total costs entering the contest. The downside is you have many of "non-winners" – people that have performed above current levels that are now not winning in the game. To ensure this does not happen, I would recommend you have a point value (i.e. 1 point each) on all duplicate tickets an employee may collect. They could then turn them in at the end of the contest for prizes (to ensure we reward good performance) or use them for a program-ending auction.

SALES TIPS

WHERE WE ARE TODAY

Since a large portion of this book is geared around creating a recognition culture by focusing on the performer who is driving sales and profits, you will need to give your team some tips on how to do these things, not just telling them to do it. Much has been written about selling and sales tactics over the years, both good and bad. The current philosophy is getting away from the bored, scripted things you see with many sales people today:

RESTAURANTS

"Hi, welcome to _____, would you like to try a super jumbo extra sized value meal today?"

"How about a top shelf margarita today?"

"Save room for dessert?"

"Would you like to add a $6.95 steak to your $3.95 omelet? They make us ask!"

"If they wanted something, they'd ask – it's on the menu"

SALESPEOPLE

"Have we got the perfect car for you!"

"How much do you want to spend today?"

"What would you like your payments to be?"

"Would you like a new _____ credit card today?"

"Would you like the $49.99 extended warranty for that $29 telephone?"

APPENDIX B

THE NEW APPROACH

The new approach you are hearing and reading about is more of a 'read-and-sell' philosophy. By that, I mean the server, cashier or salesperson being able to read the guest/client and steering them through their experience based on the type of guest/client they are. All too often, guests may take selling the wrong way – they feel like we are trying to add on to their cost at every opportunity (i.e. appetizers, dessert, credit applications, car options and warranties).

Companies have set policies and procedures mandating pushy selling to everyone. Is the short-term sales dollar worth more than the long-term value of a guest? If your wheel is balanced, the long-term benefit will prevail. If the wheel is too focused on short-term sales and profits, chances are you will discount the long-term value of the guest – and lose employees. Take a more focused approach – sell those items that you think a specific type of person would like. After all, if someone comes in with a coupon, they are probably a little cost-sensitive and would not appreciate a hard sell for a lot of suggested add-ons – especially the expensive ones.

Think about your last car buying experience for a minute. When you went in to buy a car, they did not start you off on the base model and then try to add on the options – did they? They know if you are looking at a $20,000 car and they try to add on all these options, you will feel like you are spending more money. Suggestive selling can be viewed the same way. The car dealer will put you into the $30,000 model that is fully loaded and then you take out the things you do not want. You see the value in many of the features you were not aware of when you walked into the showroom.

You feel better spending $25,000 in the second scenario than $24,000 in the first. Many people actually feel like they 'saved money' when the experience was over. All businesses would love their guests or clients to spend more, but feel like they spent less. Start with the "loaded package" of your product and work backwards. Include the warranty, the larger quantity size for a price break, the larger portion food, and then work backwards – would you like to save a little money? While some people will downsize, you will still sell far more than working up from the bottom.

You can't expect to drive your business by thinking your guest/client will always make the ideal purchase. You need to assist them along the way. Visit Red, Hot N Blue (the barbecue chain). They identify first time diners and offer a small sample (free) of their most popular, expensive and misunderstood (and surely profitable) items. What a great way to give the guest something extra to entice them to spend more!

My challenge to fast food restaurants is this: They sell value meals (great deals for their guests) and then try to 'upsize' them. How many of their employees even ask if you would like to super size, jumbo size, upsize, king size or whatever they call it? Most fast food restaurants average about 10%-12% upgrades of these meals – think their cashiers are asking? Sure looks like their managers need to finish reading this book and implement some of these ideas into their operations. Option #1 would be to incentivize their cashiers to sell more. Another option could be to sell the meal already upsized and let you downsize it and save 49 cents (Car Dealer Philosophy). The consumer will feel like they are saving money if you downsize, and I guarantee the restaurant will raise their sales much higher than the 10%-12% rate they currently realize today!

Whatever product you sell or service you deliver, you can take the same approach. Develop, package or market your line of products to make it easier for your sales force to sell them. Then incentivize those that perform. Everyone wins in that scenario. Retail chains can give rewards to the employees and managers who sell the most. Car rental companies can reward phone agents who get guests to upgrade their car level or desk agents who add on coverage. Hotel chains can reward front desk personnel for upgrading guests to a nicer and more expensive room.

You need to instill that philosophy into your sellers, but only when the time is right – for example, a first time visitor to your restaurant (e.g. Red, Hot N Blue). If you work in a hotel, you will not offer a $25 room upgrade to someone on a very discounted rate – they are definitely giving you the message that price is an issue with them, so you will not want to try to sell them the "loaded package."

'READ-AND-SELL'

'Read-and-sell' is focusing your sales effort in a targeted "rifle-shot" approach (focus on key opportunities where the odds are good), versus a "shotgun blast" (if you keep firing, eventually something will get hit).

The strategy about to be described enables your sales team to have this focused approach because of the opportunity to capitalize on the following. Since we all eat out, we'll use a restaurant example for simplicity's sake. You can equate the same scenario to your business environment.

A TALE OF TWO QUESOS

Let me share a story with you about my favorite casual dining chain. I love chips and hot sauce and overall this chain does a great job nationwide, except... about three years ago, they began offering two different types of queso (cheese dip). It should be a no-brainer for the servers to sell this item to any guest who orders chips and hot sauce ('Read-and-sell' – they are already ordering this item and the queso is a natural add-on).

I've literally eaten at over 100 of their restaurants and never had anyone offer it: "Sir, we offer two awesome choices of queso, which one would you like?" It would generate them an additional $2, and it is an easy sell for the server versus "Would you like an appetizer tonight?" No cannibalization of sales of other items, just a huge opportunity when they were averaging about a ten percent add-on rate of these items (of the guests who ordered chips and hot sauce). Needless to say, the products went away due to slow sales. Was it an inferior product or lack of execution?

They had the right idea on the menu, but the focus at the operational level was not there. Therefore, they did not move the great product they had. Incentivize your sellers to follow this strategy and they will reap huge rewards. Additionally, this lack of selling solidifies the theory that cash does not motivate. A server would receive 30 cents extra in tips for each order sold, yet they rarely did!

Ultimately one of the products went away. If the marketing department had put a few dollars into 'incentivizing' the servers and hostesses to promote it, not only would that item still be on the menu today, but their sales would be higher as well. They should have had the vendor participate in supplying prizes and awards for the managers and servers to jumpstart the sales of these products. Everyone would have won in the end, including the guest!

The sales department needs the marketing department and vice versa. How many great products have gone by the way side due to either inadequate marketing, or more importantly, poor execution at the sales or operational level. Do not take a chance – put a few of the advertising dollars on the front line and watch what happens to the top and bottom lines!

"WOULD YOU LIKE?" vs. "WHICH ONE WOULD YOU LIKE?"

Typically, you hear the following suggestive selling methods (if you're lucky to hear any at all):

"Would you like dessert tonight?"   "Would you like the warranty?"

"Would you like to upsize that?"   "Would you like a larger car today?"

"Would you like a margarita tonight?"   "Would you like to apply for credit?"

"Would you like extra cheese on that pizza?"   "Would you like a suite upgrade?"

"Do you want cheese on that hamburger?"   "Can I get you an appetizer?"

What is the problem with the approach? The good news is that they are asking, but the bad news is it does not work frequently enough. The odds are stacked against you. How many ways can you answer the question?

QUESTION:
"Would you like the extended warranty with that $699 PC today?"

ANSWER	POSITIVE RESPONSE?
"YES"	Yes
"NO"	No
"How much is it?"	Potentially
"Is there more than 1 kind?"	No
"What does it include?"	No
"Does it cover everything?"	No

There are too many negative answers to the question you are asking!

The odds are only one in six you will get a positive response – with one potential "yes". Additionally, by asking this question to every guest, you have not read them and have no idea if they are interested in even buying that item (shotgun approach). While you may increase short-term results, it will be at the expense of sacrificing the long-term value of the guest. It is no different than maintaining your car – if you skip the oil changes today, you save money now, but you are setting yourself up for a very large expense in the future. Now, change the question and ask it a different way.

"With the three year all-inclusive warranty, the total is $799. We also have a two-year warranty that would lower the total to $749. Without the warranty, the total would be $699. Which one would you like?"

ANSWER	POSITIVE RESPONSE?
3 Year Warranty	Yes – Extra $100 in Sales
2 Year Warranty	Yes – Extra $50 in Sales
No Warranty	No

You have greatly increased your odds of success for 2 reasons:

1) You are only asking this question in a manner that presents many options for them and it appears you are offering to save them some money.

2) You are asking the question in the way that there are more positive answers!

Many companies have tried all kinds of sales pitches. They are either too 'hard-sell' on the guest, or the employee does not go the extra step since they are either uncomfortable asking (lack of training) or not gaining anything extra for themselves while driving the business (wheel out of balance). Teach them the subtleties and then reward them for helping with the sales!

SELLING OPPORTUNITIES TO DRIVE SALES

- Offer packaged deals – Fast food created the niche (sandwich, fries and a drink). Bundle your services and sell as a package. Not only would it provide a better value to the guest or client, it provides more direction to the sales force to sell. You would think movie theaters would be all over this one – large popcorn and two medium drinks (with the upsell to large drinks for only $___ extra). Include the warranty in the price of the item.

- Offer the middle or higher level option first and then work backwards. This is ideal for service industries, hotels (ocean view room versus standard view) or fast food restaurants to sell the value meal already upsized – and offer to save money if they want to downsize it (discussed earlier).

- Offer two different car or room upgrades ("which one would you like") to a guest renting a car or hotel room.

- Sell the product with the warranty built in and ask the guest if they would like to 'save' some money by taking that off the price. Then they feel like they are getting a better deal, as well as being made aware of all the potential options.

- Offer more than 1 size of what you sell (i.e. case packs, price levels) – instead of asking everyone "would you like a ____?" your sales force can ask "which one would you like?"

- Offer side items or add-on services for a reduced price off the regular. For example, you could have a "garden salad" on the menu for $2.75, but offer a dinner salad (slightly smaller) with any burger/sandwich for only $1.29. The warranty might be $10 less if you spend over a certain limit. Again, this provides focus for the salesperson – only those ordering these items would get this suggestion.

- Offer two different warranties – a short time period and a longer one. Again, more than 1 potential "yes" answer vs. "would you like the warranty?"

- Offer choices of the same item (like queso) – Server must execute the sales opportunity here though – "Which one would you like?" vs. "Would you like?" If you just suggest a different appetizer each time, you cannibalize sales of another – nothing incremental is gained.

INDEX

INDEX

NOTES

NOTES